S·E·W·I·N·G
LUNA LAPIN'S FRIENDS

Sarah Peel

With short stories by Grace Machon

DAVID & CHARLES

www.davidandcharles.com

FOREWORD

Luna Lapin, our original rabbitty-hare, was created in 2013 as a muse for the tiny clothing designs that were in my head. Since then Luna has become quite a global celebrity and has her own book, Making Luna Lapin. Of course, such a kind rabbit was always going to have friends, and this book teaches you to make them and their stylish, interchangeable clothing. We don't regard the animals as toys, they are more heirloom pieces, or an indulgence for all of us who are still children at heart. We hope you enjoy Luna's little world.

Sarah

CONTENTS

Luna
AND THE
fine old thing

When Luna Lapin was a kitten she spent Tuesdays with her Granny. Granny Rabbit was a sweet old thing who walked with a single cane and had the largest collection of scarves known to rabbitkind. Luna loved her dearly, and always looked forward to their time together. Granny had many projects and her house brimmed with old books and fabric, some older than herself, which for a little rabbit seemed quite nearly impossible.

Luna loved to hear stories of where these beautiful things had come from. There was smooth, cold cotton from Egypt, ribbons that had been saved from birthday cakes and clippings of lace from wedding dresses. Metres of silk that slipped through the fingers like liquid, and the most wonderful assortment of prints you wouldn't even begin to imagine.

Granny Rabbit's house was a treasure trove of imagination, so much so Luna truly believed that fairies sipped the milk left on the bird table for them overnight and that the mice that lived there really did steal Granny's glasses.

One day, just after Luna had gotten out of the bath, her bob tail fluffed up once more after a long day making mud pies with her naughty little brother, Granny asked Luna if she would like to learn something new. Now Luna was never one to shy away from new things so of course she said yes.

Granny's sewing machine was a fine old thing, a beautiful trio of red flowers stood out on its glossy black bow, the blooms outlined in gold. Luna had watched in wonder as Granny had picked out fabrics, laid tissue paper in all sorts of odd shapes upon them and began to cut with such great confidence and her tongue poking out of her mouth (a habit that was somewhat of a family trait). And with the beating of a foot (something that for a rabbit was quite easy) and the whirr of cogs and bobbins something amazing would soon be fashioned and slipped over little Luna's head.

Luna sat patiently as her Granny explained the best way to place your pins, how to hold the scissors so you get the cleanest, straightest line. "Now you just have to make friends with your sewing machine," Granny said. And Luna did, every Tuesday, for her little world was meant to be full of perfect choices, perfect dresses.

Materials

This section describes the materials and equipment you will need to make the projects in this book.

BEFORE YOU START

Before starting a project, look at the You Will Need list for the project and gather your supplies. Give yourself enough space and time to work – this really does help eliminate mistakes. Read through all of a project's instructions first and highlight any areas that you will need to focus on more than the simpler parts. Press fabric with a suitable iron temperature to ensure it is flat and easy to work with.

BASIC SEWING KIT

You will need some general supplies for making the projects in the book, including the following:

- Selection of needles, including sewing needle, tapestry needle, darner needle and doll needle (for sewing on arms)
- Sewing threads to suit projects, including embroidery threads
- Pins and safety pins
- Sharp scissors for fabric and scissors for paper
- Fabric marker (e.g. water-soluble pen or chalk)
- Adhesive tape
- Implement for turning parts through and stuffing (e.g. knitting needle or chopstick)
- Iron
- Sewing machine

FABRICS

Various fabric types have been used for the projects in the book and this section gives some advice on using them.

Felt

Felt is possibly the perfect crafting material. The felt I am referring to in this book is a flat fabric-like felt, not what you would use for needle-felting or wet felting. Felt is not a woven fabric, but is formed by the agitation of fibres and therefore will not fray when you cut it. This allows you to cut a shape that can be appliquéd, or sewn to the outside of a project. However, not all felts are made equal, so if possible choose a felt that has wool in it, and look for a thickness of about 1.5mm (¹⁄₁₆in) – definitely no thicker. I adore the softly marled tones of the felts that are used for Luna and her clothes, which are a wool and viscose blend (see Suppliers). Felt doesn't have a grain to the material, so you can move your pattern pieces around to get the most out of your felt.

Corduroy

Corduroy is a fabric that has a luxurious look and feel. The fabric is made up of ribs of tufted fibres, called wales. Colours seem to glow in corduroy; think of it as a practical, everyday velvet. As with all of Luna and her friends' projects, it's important to think of their scaled down world, so choose a fine needlecord (one that has 14 wales per inch – or higher).

TIPS ON SEWING WITH CORDUROY

When cutting out the corduroy, all pattern pieces should be laid up and cut in the same direction, because corduroy has a 'pile' which means it looks a different shade one way to the opposite way – our layouts follow these principles.

Wool Tweed

The beautiful soft colours and natural fibres of wool tweed make it perfect for Luna's fashionable wardrobe. Tweed is a heritage fabric and when buying it is worth researching the provenance of what you are investing in. Don't think you have to go out and buy a huge amount though – it may be you could recycle an old tweed jacket into a skirt and bag for Luna. Save scraps too, as the tiniest pieces can be used for appliqué. Avoid anything too chunky as Luna's clothes are a miniature scale, which means you need something mid-weight rather than heavy. If you are worried about matching stripes or checks, turn the fabric to be on the bias (so the pattern is diagonal) as this will give a different, less design-critical look.

Printed Fabrics

Cottons tend to be more stable than other fabric compositions and therefore will give you more control when you are sewing these small items. Choose prints that work with the scale of the garment – that's why I love the ditsy prints you will see in the projects. Choose fabrics that are lightweight without being delicate – a quilting weight is about as heavy as you should select.

Trims

There are some wonderful trims and haberdashery available, designed to make sewing easier as well as more beautiful. The most important consideration when choosing trims is scale: try to use doll buttons rather than those you would use for your own clothing. Select narrow ricrac or ribbon so it looks like it belongs in a miniature world. Be inventive – these designs are just a starting point and the best creations are of your own invention.

Techniques

This section describes the basic techniques used for the projects. Each project is given a difficulty rating with the You Will Need lists – one acorn for easy projects, working up to three acorns for more difficult ones.

LAYOUTS

Layout diagrams are given for the projects as a guide for the amount of fabric needed, but if you have a different shape of fabric you will need to be flexible. Take note of which pattern piece will need to be cut out more than once and pin this onto double thickness fabric. The pattern pieces and layouts give this information so follow them carefully.

PATTERNS

All patterns are supplied full size in a section at the back of the book called The Patterns. Please follow the guidelines there for using the patterns.

CUTTING OUT

Time spent on accurate cutting will really improve your end result. Use a good quality pair of scissors that are suitable for (and reserved for) fabric. I tend to use the part of the blades that are closer to my hand to start cutting – this gives me better control and allows me to make a longer cut, as I have the rest of the blades to travel through the fabric. I only use the tips of the scissors when I am marking notches or for really fiddly bits.

TRANSFERRING MARKINGS

Mark the notches shown on the patterns with either a tiny snip in the fabric or using a water-soluble pen or chalk marker. Mark any triangles as a triangular cut from the fabric. Mark any dots on the patterns with either a water-soluble pen or tailor's tacks. The triangles and dots are position markers. The notches can be there to mark a position or to help you ease around curves so please be accurate when you are snipping them. Once you have marked the positions, unpin the pattern pieces from the cut fabric and store them together once you are sure you have cut them all out.

RIGHT SIDE AND WRONG SIDE

Printed fabrics and some plain fabrics have a right side and a wrong side, and this is shown in the illustrations and referred to in the instructions. Felt normally has no definite right or wrong side, but I have referred to right and wrong to help you sew.

FINISHING RAW EDGES

You could use an overlocker or a machine zigzag stitch to finish the raw edges of the seams on woven fabrics. The items in this book are small ones that are not going to be washed, so this is optional. Because of the nature of felt, the edges do not need finishing.

HAND SEWING STITCHES

Hand sewing is relaxing, portable and allows you to focus on something creative. Luna's friends are sewn by hand and you could aim to complete a limb each night or perhaps take her on your commute to work. I have used various stitches, both practical and pretty. Always start and finish with either a knot in the fabric or a couple of small stitches in the same place.

Overstitch / Whipstitch

I use an overstitch (also called whipstitch) to sew felt pieces together. Use a single thread thickness and make sure you sew consistently, that is, the same distance between stitches and the same depth in from the edge, about 2mm (1/16in) into the felt.

Bring the needle through to the front and then sew from back to front, repeating and working from right to left if you are right-handed (see **Fig. 1**) or left to right if you are left-handed. As you pull the thread through you will feel the tension as the thread is drawn and you can then continue to the next stitch. The thread will sink into the felt.

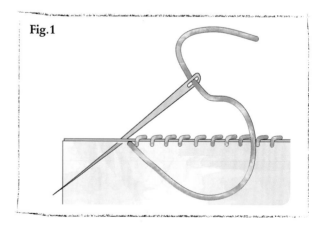

Fig. 1

Backstitch

Backstitch is used to sew two pieces of fabric or felt together with a seam allowance. Backstitch is a good replacement for machine sewing if you wish to sew the garments by hand. Use a single toning sewing thread on your needle.

Following **Fig.2**, bring the needle up at point 1 and then back to point 2. Bring it out at the top again beyond point 1 at point 3, and then back through at point 4, which should be very close to or in the same place as point 1. Repeat along the seam.

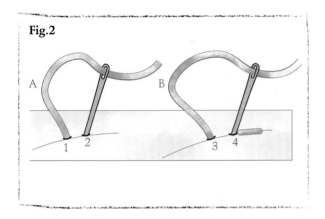

Fig.2

Blanket Stitch

Blanket stitch is a decorative and functional stitch that can be used to make a seam and to decorate it at the same time. The key to a good blanket stitch is consistency in the depth of the stitch and the distance between the stitches. A common mistake is to make the stitch too close to the edge of the fabric, which loses the decorative quality. Use a contrast embroidery thread to work blanket stitch – I tend to use between three and six strands of embroidery thread, depending on how bold you want the contrast stitch to look.

Following **Fig.3**, bring the needle through to front at point 1. Insert the needle in the front at point 2 and come out at the back at point 3, holding the thread under the needle at point 3 as you pull the stitch tight.

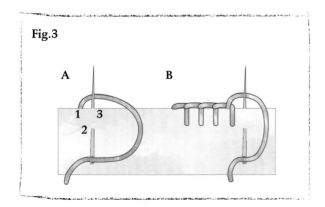

Fig.3

Satin Stitch

Satin stitch is an embroidery stitch that is good for creating blocked-out shapes in contrast colours. Use between three and six strands of the embroidery thread, depending on how bold you want the contrast stitch to look.

Following **Fig.4**, draw out the outline of the shape you are going to fill. Use the needle to pass backwards and forwards from outline to opposite outline. Try to keep your stitches parallel to one another and don't pull the stitches too tight.

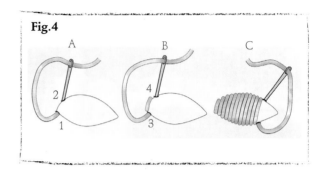

Fig.4

Slip Stitch / Ladder Stitch

A slip stitch (also called ladder stitch) is used to join two fabrics when you don't want the stitches to show.

Following **Fig.5**, secure the thread onto a bulkier part of the project – a seam allowance or the fold of a hem. Now pass your needle through a tiny amount of the main fabric and then travel diagonally into the back of the other fabric piece. Come down directly into the main fabric again, pick up a small amount again and travel diagonally across to the second fabric again. Repeat along the edge.

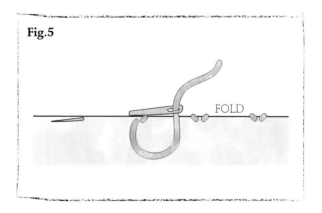

Fig.5

FOLD

MACHINE SEWING TECHNIQUES

I recommend sewing the clothes for Luna and her friends on a sewing machine as this will give a more professional and even finish. For these projects it is assumed that you have the basic skills of machine sewing. However, here are a few tips on how to sew small items.

The Right Stitch

Test your fabrics first, for example, a cotton lawn will react differently to a tweed under the machine and you may need to adjust the stitch length or tension.

'Donkey' or Stitch Starter

If you find that with small projects and fine fabrics your fabric tends to disappear down into the needle plate at the start of a seam, you could use what's called a donkey. Fold over a piece of scrap fabric so it's about 5cm (2in) square and a few layers thick and start your line of sewing on this. Butt the project up to the donkey and continue sewing onto the project – reversing as in Securing Your Stitching, below, but without involving the donkey. You can snip the threads to detach the donkey at the end of the seam and use it again and again.

Securing Your Stitching

Always use your machine reverse function to start and finish seams as this will stop your seams from coming undone. The reversing should only be for two to three stitches – if you stitch any more than this then you probably will have lost the line of stitching anyway.

Seam Allowance

It is amazing how many people come to my Make Friends with Your Sewing Machine classes who don't know what the little parallel grooves are on the footplate of the sewing machine. These are your sewing guidelines and before you start sewing you should identify which line is right for the recommended seam allowance. So, if sewing with a 1cm (⅜in) seam allowance, you should be feeding the sewing through the machine so the raw edges are on the right-hand side of the presser foot and are running along the 10mm groove. If you are working to a narrow 0.5cm (¼in) seam allowance, use the edge of your presser foot as the guide for the edge of the fabric.

Using the Hand Wheel

Instead of using the foot pedal, using your hand wheel to make the last few stitches before a point you are aiming for can really improve your accuracy and confidence. Always turn the wheel towards you.

Turning a Corner

To make a crisp, accurate 90-degree corner when you are sewing, at the point of the corner leave the needle down in the fabric, lift the presser foot and move the fabric around at a 90-degree angle, and then continue sewing.

Coping with Curves

Sewing a curve is easier if you are using your seam guidelines. Slow down to control your sewing more easily and if you need to realign what you are doing, leave the needle down in the fabric, lift the presser foot and move the fabric slightly to bring the curve back in line. You may find that you have a speed setting on your machine or foot pedal, so if it helps you should slow the speed down whilst you practise new techniques.

Easing

There are times when it feels like you are squeezing more fabric on one side to match less fabric on another side. This can occur, for example, if you are setting in a sleeve or sewing a curve onto a straight piece of fabric. To help with easing there are two different techniques, as follows.

METHOD 1:

This is the normal dressmaking technique. Change your stitch length to be the longest possible. Do not reverse at the beginning or end, and then on the longer looking side (normally the curved side), sew two rows of stitching. Row 1 should be 3mm (⅛in) from the raw edge. Row 2 should be 6mm (¼in). Now grab the sewing threads from one end of the upper side of the fabric and gently pull to slightly gather up the fabric. Do the same with the other ends, but make sure you don't have actual gathers, just more tightness. Now you can pin and sew to the other piece of fabric and eventually remove the initial stitching. Remember to change your stitch length back to normal first though.

METHOD 2:

This is the factory method. Take the tighter (usually the straighter piece of fabric) and put snips 1cm (⅜in) apart along the edge of the fabric, which are a little bit shorter than the seam allowance allowed. This will lengthen the edge of the fabric and allow it to stretch to the longer curved piece.

Staystitching

Staystitching is a foundation step to keep your fabric from stretching. Sew using a normal length straight stitch just inside the given seam allowance so that your stitches will be hidden. Sew without reversing at the beginning or end of your sewing so that you can easily remove the stitches if necessary.

Edgestitch

An edgestitch is a line of stitching that is very close, about 1mm–2mm ($\frac{1}{32}$in–$\frac{1}{16}$in) away from a seam or folded edge. It is used to decorate or strengthen a seam. An easy way of establishing a guideline for edgestitching is to move your needle across to the left-hand position and then use the groove in the centre of the presser foot as your seam guideline. Stitch slowly to keep the stitching even.

Topstitch

A topstitch is a line of stitching that is close, about 4mm–5mm ($\frac{3}{16}$in) away from a seam or folded edge. It is used to decorate or strengthen a seam. Use the edge of the presser foot as your seam guideline. Edgestitching and topstitching can be used together to create a twin needling effect.

Gathering

Gathering is a decorative effect, allowing a longer piece of fabric to be suppressed into a shorter piece of fabric. It creates a pretty effect and can create shaping in a garment.

To gather, change your machine stitch to be at its longest, or to the gathering setting. Following **Fig.6**, sew along the top edge 0.5cm ($\frac{1}{4}$in) down and then repeat the line of stitching 1cm ($\frac{3}{8}$in) down. It is important that you don't reverse or fasten your threads off at this stage. Take the two top threads from one end, and firmly but steadily pull the threads so the material moves along and gathers. Repeat with the top threads at the other end and gather up the fabric to the specified length. Tie off the ends of the thread to secure the gathering or wind in a figure of eight around a pin. I cannot stress enough how valuable it is to spend time getting your gathers evenly distributed along the fabric. When you have sewn the fabrics together as instructed for each garment, the original gathering threads can be pulled out.

Press as You Go

An iron is as valuable to the sewing process as the sewing machine itself. If possible, and depending on the shape, set the seam first by pressing the seam flat. Then open up the fabric and use the nose of the iron to either open up the seam allowances and press flat, or to flatten the seam allowances together in one direction. Your fingers will be working near the hot iron so do take care.

Making Buttonholes

Buttonholes are a finishing touch to garments and an important fastening function BUT in this tiny world, it might be difficult for your sewing machine to create buttonholes. So have a think about your capabilities, practise on your machine with some scrap fabric and most importantly, remember it would be a horrible thing to have got almost to the end of making the clothes to then make a mess of the buttonholes. If you are having a go, a sewing machine with either a computerised function (where you can put in the length of buttonhole required) will work, as will machines where you turn a knob for each stage of the buttonhole. A machine which has a foot where the button drops into the back to determine the buttonhole length will not work – the button is too small to be detected. Once the buttonhole is completed, cut through the small area between the zigzag stitches carefully using an unpicker. To do this safely, place pins at each far end of the buttonhole, but just before the wide end bar of stitching. This will stop the unpicker from cutting further. If you don't want to try machine buttonholes, you could always embroider the detail on using a satin stitch, or just use buttons and snap fasteners.

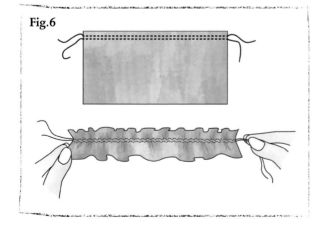

Fig.6

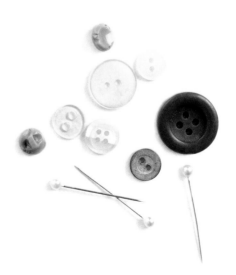

The fox
AND HIS father

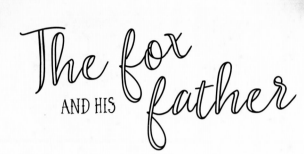

Ralph Reynard's father was a true red fox, his bushy tail a hunter's dream. Proud, almost haughty, Reynard's father had ideas of what it meant to be a fox and Reynard did not fit this mould. He had no time for the romping and running that filled his siblings' days. He was not a sly fox, or a shy fox. He was the best dressed fox, the sharpest fox, you could even say the smartest fox.

Reynard leaned back in his chair, papers strewn all over his desk. Today marked the fifth year as editor at the magazine, and six years since his father's death. Reynard stroked his fine tail. All more than worth it he thought, remembering the hard work it took to get from errand boy to this chair. Reynard took his old man's jacket off the hook; it still held the stern look of his father, pockets full of what his dad believed made a good fox. Reynard hoped he was all those things. He remembered the long drive they had taken to the city all those years ago. On his first day at La Clairière, his father had handed him the jacket off his own back and said, "This is the nicest thing I have, but I think you need it more than I do. Be great, son." Reynard remembered his father's grey flecked face and that his laugh was always too loud. There wasn't a day he didn't miss him.

The jacket was all Reynard had left of his father, and there was no doubt it brought him luck. Reynard thought back to his first assignment as a junior writer. Our foxy friend had been walking aimlessly around backstage at a fashion show, hoping he would bump into someone who was someone. Reynard sat down and began to twiddle the shining brass buttons on his father's old jacket. One of the buttons came off in his hand – it popped across the room! This was a disaster! Reynard was fast, but not as fast as a flying button.

He watched in dismay as the button soared over the heads of the fashionable and fancy. It landed with a plop in a glass of fizzing elderflower. What on earth was Reynard to do? He would need all his foxy cunning to spare him from this great embarrassment, or worse! What if this glamorous lady choked; he would never get over it!

Reynard snuck to the waiters' table and acted like he belonged, taking a tray of glasses, and began to work the room, collecting empties and offering refreshments. Thank goodness the red haired lady didn't drink very quickly. Reynard never let her leave his sight. Finally he reached her, he was about to take her glass and then…

"Hey! I'm not done with that!" the bright young thing said. Reynard tried to back away, the room was too full of movement. He slipped and glasses went everywhere, covering everyone around in sticky sweet fizz. Reynard began to panic, to many it was only a button but it was so much more to Reynard.

He began to mumble apologies and try to explain, expecting no one to care about the single brass button like he did. He had forgotten these are fashion folk! The lady with the red hair dropped to her knees and began to search.

"I've got it!" she shouted, holding the shiny speck in her hand. You may be wondering at this point how on earth this could possibly be a lucky jacket, but the red haired lady was none other than Mae Loveday, stylist to the stars (and future in-house stylist of La Clairière) and the best friend any fox could wish for.

There was a knock at the door and a rabbit walked in. "Are you okay? It's just that we are waiting for you on these proofs," Luna handed him the little black book containing the next issue of Reynard's beloved magazine. "Of course, of course," he said, "I'll get to it."

Reynard's Tweed Jacket

YOU WILL NEED

- **30cm (11¾in) x 75cm (29½in) 100% wool tweed for main fabric**
- **30cm (11¾in) x 75cm (29½in) light to quilting weight 100% cotton for lining**
- **Two 8mm (⁵⁄₁₆in) metal buttons**
- **Basic sewing kit (see Materials)**

Use a 0.5cm (¼in) seam allowance, unless a different amount is stated.

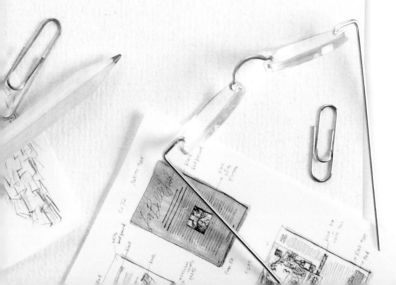

CUTTING OUT

1 Cut around your paper pattern pieces for the jacket carefully using scissors. I like to cut on the black line, but to the outside not the inside.

2 For the outer jacket, fold the tweed fabric in half with right sides together. Pin your pattern pieces onto the fabric using **Fig.1** as a guide. Cut all pieces as stated on the pattern. Mark any triangles with a small snip to the centre. Mark the small dot to help you position the pocket flap on the jacket front and the button and buttonhole positions using tailor's tacks or a water-soluble pen.

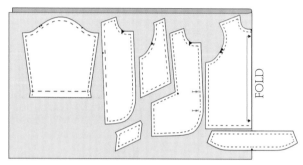

Fig.1

3 For the jacket lining, fold the lining fabric in half with right sides together and cut out the same way you did the main (outer) fabric using **Fig.2** as a guide.

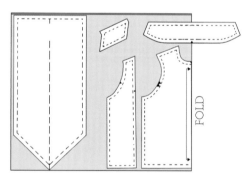

Fig.2

MAKING UP

Making the Pocket Flaps:

1 With right sides together, match one outer pocket flap with one lining pocket flap. Pin and sew around three sides, leaving the long top edge open (see Machine Sewing Techniques: Turning a Corner) (**Fig.3**).

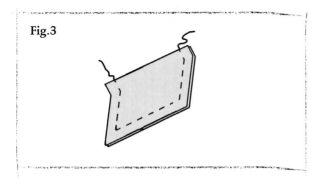

Fig.3

2 Repeat with remaining pocket flap pieces – making sure you have a pair rather than two identical pocket flaps. Trim the excess fabric from the corners (**Fig.4**).

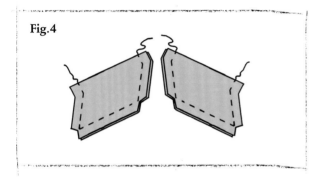

Fig.4

3 Turn through, rolling seams out to the edges between your fingers and make sure you have pushed the corners out. Press flat with a warm iron.

Sewing the Pocket Flaps to the Jacket Front:

1 Take the two jacket front pieces and lay in front of you right sides up. Position a pocket flap on each front referring to the pocket position markings on your pattern piece. Make sure the top edge of the pocket matches the upper edge of the front and that the notches match. Tack (baste) into position (**Fig.5**).

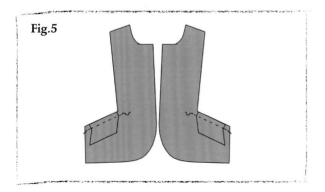

Fig.5

Sewing the Jacket Side Front to the Jacket Front:

1 With right sides together, take one side front and place the lower edge across the front pocket line (sandwiching the pocket flap between the front and side front). Pin in place and sew taking care to stop sewing 0.5cm (¼in) away from the end closest to the curved opening edge of the jacket front (**Fig.6**). This will match up with the spot you marked on the front when you were cutting out your pieces.

2 Now flip the pieces over so you are looking at the wrong side of the front and snip into the corner you marked on the front (**Fig.7**).

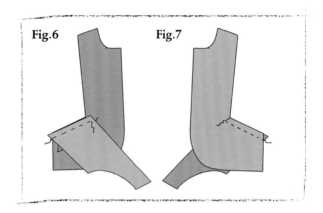

Fig.6   **Fig.7**

3 Open out the front edge and sew to the side front. Repeat with other side (**Fig.8**). Press the upper seams open and flat.

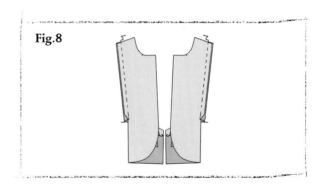

Fig.8

Sewing the Front Facing to the Front Lining:

1 With right sides together, sew one front facing to one front lining, matching notches (**Fig.9**). Press seam open. Repeat with other front facing and front lining (**Fig.10**).

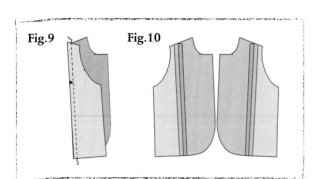

Fig.9   Fig.10

Sewing the Shoulder Seams in the Outer and Lining:

1 With right sides together, match the shoulder seam of one front to one back shoulder seam and sew together. Repeat with the other front and the remaining back shoulder seam and press seams open (**Fig.11**).

2 With right sides together, match the shoulder seam of one front facing/lining to one back shoulder seam and sew together. Repeat with the other front facing/lining and the remaining back shoulder seam. Press seams open (**Fig.12**).

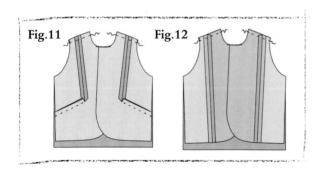

Fig.11   Fig.12

Sewing the Sleeves:

1 Finish the raw edge of the sleeve hem using an overlocker or zigzag stitch on your machine. Hem the sleeves by turning 1cm (⅜in) to the wrong side. Press and sew in place through all layers (**Fig.13**).

Fig.13

2 With right sides together, match one sleeve to the armhole using the notches to position. Pin in place and sew together. Repeat with other sleeve. Press seam allowance towards sleeve (**Fig.14**).

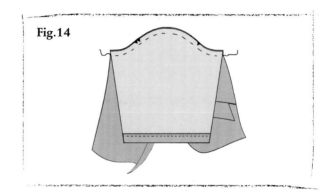

Fig.14

Sewing the Side Seams:

1 With right sides together, match up the sleeve seams, underarm and side seams of the main jacket and pin in place. Sew the under sleeve and side seam in one go. Press seams open as far as you can (**Fig.15**).

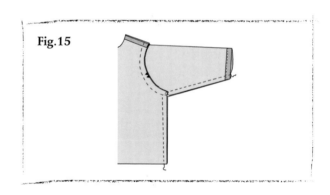

Fig.15

2 Repeat with side seams on the lining (there are no sleeves in the lining), press seams open (**Fig.16**).

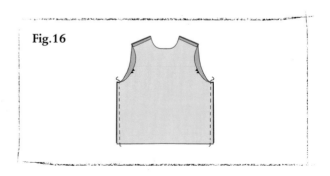

Fig.16

Making the Collar:

1 With right sides together, pin the two collar pieces (one lining, one outer) together, matching the corners and sew along the two short ends and the long un-notched edge (**Fig.17**).

2 Trim the corners to reduce the bulk when you turn through (**Fig.18**).

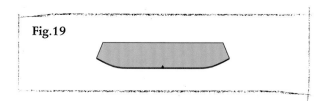

Fig.17   **Fig.18**

3 Turn through and press flat, ensuring the seams are right on the edge (**Fig.19**).

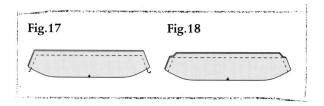

Fig.19

Sewing the Collar and Lining to the Jacket:

1 With the right side of the outer jacket facing you, place the collar with wool side face up onto the neck edge of the jacket. Position it so that the edges of the collar line up with the notches on the front and match the rest of the collar up with the neckline, using centre back notch as guide. Pin, then tack (baste) in place (**Fig.20**) .

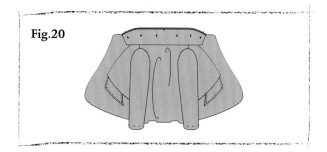

Fig.20

2 Take the lining and place it onto the outer jacket with the right sides of both layers touching, matching the notches around the neck edge and the curve of the front edge, side seams, etc. Pin in place all the way around the jacket – making sure the sleeves are tucked inside. Starting at one lower front edge, sew all the way around the pinned edge (**Fig.21**).

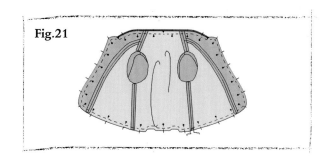

Fig.21

3 Trim any corners to reduce bulk and trim the neck seam allowance back to be 0.25cm (⅛in) deep. Turn the jacket right side out by gradually feeding the fabric through one lining armhole. Roll the seams to be at the outside and press flat with a warm iron.

FINISHING OFF

1 After pressing all the edges, edgestitch (see Machine Sewing Techniques: Edgestitch) around the front edge of the jacket from the side seam around the front of the coat, pivoting at the lapel, around the collar and down the other front, finishing at the other side seam (**Fig.22**).

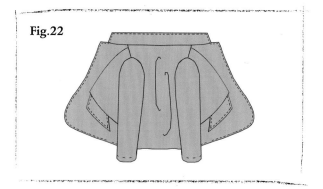

Fig.22

2 Oversew the lining armholes to the seam allowance of the sleeve armhole.

3 If you are not confident with making buttonholes, practise on some scrap wool. It would be a horrible thing to have got this far with the jacket to then make a mess of the buttonholes (see Machine Sewing Techniques: Making Buttonholes). Make buttonholes on left-hand side front (as worn) using positions marked on the pattern. Sew buttons onto the right-hand side front.

4 Using a warm iron press the lapels down so the break point (where the lapels start to fold back) is level with the first buttonhole.

Reynard's Breeches

CUTTING OUT

1 Cut around your paper pattern pieces for the breeches carefully using scissors. I like to cut on the black line, but to the outside not the inside.

2 Fold the cord fabric in half with right sides together, so that the lines in the cord run along the length of the pattern. Pin your pattern pieces onto the fabric using **Fig.1** as a guide. Cut all pieces as stated on the pattern. Mark any triangles with a small snip to the centre. Mark the X and the dot at the hem to help you make the pleat and position the buttons, using tailor's tacks or a water-soluble pen.

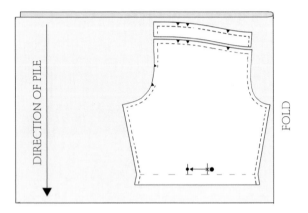

Fig.1

YOU WILL NEED

- **30cm (11¾in) x 50cm (19¾in) 100% cotton needlecord**
- **Two 8mm (⁵⁄₁₆in) metal buttons**
- **22cm (8½in) of 0.5cm (¼in) wide elastic**
- **Basic sewing kit (see Materials)**

Use a 0.5cm (¼in) seam allowance, unless a different amount is stated.

MAKING UP

Sewing the Hems:

1 Finish the raw edge of the breeches hem using an overlocker or zigzag stitch on your machine. Hem the legs by turning 1.5cm (⅝in) to the wrong side. Press and sew through all layers. Repeat with other leg (**Fig.2**).

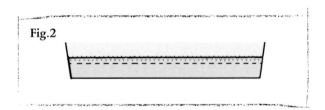

Fig.2

Sewing the Inside Legs:

1 Working one leg at a time, fold each leg in half along length with right sides together, match the inside leg seams and sew (**Fig.3**).

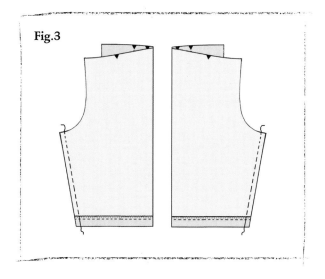

Fig.3

Sewing the Crotch:

1 Turn one leg right side out and slide it, hem first, inside the other leg so that the right sides are touching to sew the crotch. Matching edges and notches and inside leg seams, pin and sew the crotch. Leave an opening in the seam for the tail between the two notches (**Fig.4**).

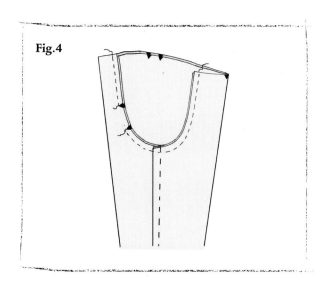

Fig.4

Making the Waist Facing:

1 With right sides together, sew together the short ends of the two waist facing pieces and press open (**Fig.5**).

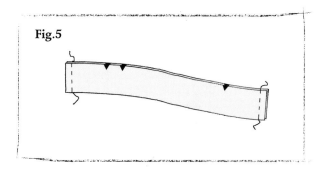

Fig.5

2 The facing will now be a circular loop. Finish the un-notched edge of the waist facing using an overlocker or zigzag stitch on your machine (**Fig.6**).

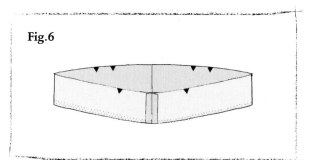

Fig.6

Sewing the Waist and Casing:

1 With the breeches right side out, place the waist facing over the waist of the breeches with the right sides together, match up the edges of the waist to the facing using the notches (there are single notches along the front waist and double notches along the back), match the centre front and centre back seams and sew the facing to the breeches (**Fig.7**).

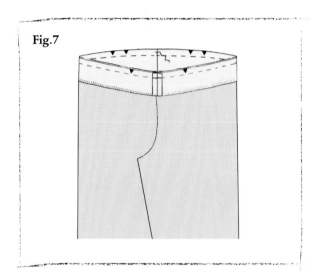

Fig.7

2 Turn the facing to the inside of the breeches, press and pin in place. Edgestitch around the top edge (see Machine Sewing Techniques: Edgestitch). Topstitch 1cm (⅜in) down from the edgestitching, starting at the centre back (see Machine Sewing Techniques: Topstitch). Leave a small opening for threading in the elastic (**Fig.8**).

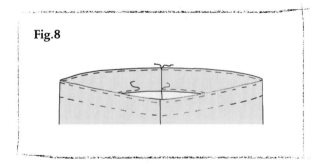

Fig.8

3 Take your elastic and pop a safety pin through one end and close the pin.

4 Thread the elastic through the casing using your safety pin, ensuring that the unthreaded end of the elastic is still accessible.

5 Overlap the two elastic ends by 2.5cm (1in) and join using a zigzag machine stitch. Pull the waistband out and the joined ends of the elastic will disappear into the casing.

6 Close the opening you left for the casing with machine stitching.

Making the Pleated Hems:

1 Working one leg at a time and using your pattern pieces to guide you, mark the pleat positions on the outside leg (**Fig.9**).

2 Bring the X to match the dot. Press and pin, then hand sew a button through all layers to hold pleat in place (**Fig.10**).

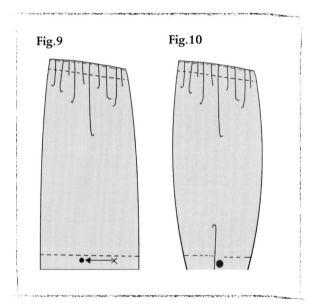

Fig.9   **Fig.10**

Reynard's Cravat

YOU WILL NEED

- **100% cotton lining (quantity is included in Reynard's Tweed Jacket lining)**
- **Basic sewing kit (see Materials)**

Use a 0.5cm (¼in) seam allowance, unless a different amount is stated.

CUTTING OUT

1 Cut around your paper pattern piece for the cravat carefully using scissors. I like to cut on the black line, but to the outside not the inside.

2 Pin your pattern piece onto the fabric using the layout for Reynard's Tweed Jacket lining as a guide. Cut all pieces as stated on the pattern.

MAKING UP

Sewing the Centre Back Seam:

1 With right sides together, pin the two cravat pieces together along the short back edges and sew. Press seam open (**Fig.1**).

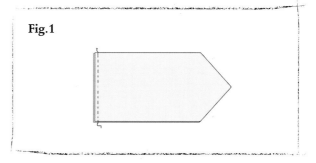

Fig.1

2 With right sides together fold the cravat in half along the length, so that the long edges match and sew. Leave a 5cm (2in) opening along the long edge for turning through (**Fig.2**).

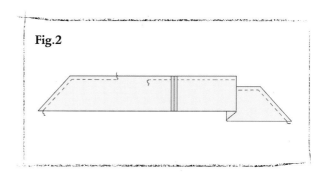

Fig.2

3 Trim off corners and turn through to right side through the seam opening. Roll edges to outside and press. Slip stitch opening together (see Hand Sewing Stitches: Slip Stitch).

Luna AND THE brand new friend

Somewhere in a sleepy hollow, Freddie was just opening his eyes. It was a slow kind of morning, full of crocuses and daffodils. Snow had lightly fallen through the night, leaving a white kiss on the path. Freddie pulled on his dungarees, the soft twill paired perfectly with his shirt.

Today was going to be a special day for Freddie. It had been many moons since he had seen Ralph Reynard.

Reynard had called him the week before and asked if he could use the farm for a photo shoot. Freddie was feeling very nervous to have all these high-flying types in his humble space. He had scrubbed down the gates and trimmed the hedges.

Freddie was cleaning out his hens when cars began to arrive.

"Freddie!" Reynard exclaimed, arms open as he walked towards his childhood friend. "How are you, old boy?"

A pretty rabbit followed him.

"You must meet Luna, you will just adore each other."

"Hello! It's so beautiful here," said the long-eared rabbit in her patchwork scarf. "It reminds me of home."

Freddie felt more at ease than he had all morning. Luna had that effect on people, you see.

The three of them made their way to the sweet little kitchen and drank tea together. Freddie was pleased to see that all kinds of folks are not immune to the charms of a homely sweet brew.

"Our Queen arrives," muttered Reynard with a roll of his eyes. "She is fantastic at what she does, Freddie! You are going to want to see this!"

Persephone pulled up, with the back of her gleaming white car covered in a thick layer of mud.

"What back water have you brought me to this time, Raffy?!?!" Reynard squirmed at this abbreviation of his name.

"Lovely to see you, Persephone. Meet Freddie – this is his farm and he's been kind enough to lend it to us, don't you think? And, of course, you know Luna – she will be the photographer for the day."

Luna waved. She was so nervous, as this was only her third photo shoot and Persephone was a very famous model, though notoriously difficult.

Persephone looked magnificent in all of the clothing, her perfect curled ears framing her face. She was a spectacular-looking poodle, even if she was all froth and frills.

The shoot was going well. Luna snapped away happily until suddenly there was a crack – the branch of the old apple tree Persephone had been leaning against gave way.

Everybody gasped as there was a big splash! Persephone lost her footing and tumbled head over heels into the duck pond. Freddie rushed forward to aid the yapping poodle.

"Why me?" she blubbered.

It was the final dress, and it had been ruined in the murky waters. But Luna had an idea – she picked up her camera and began to take pictures of the handsome badger in his smart quilted gilet. The orange detailing against his sweet country face was a stark contrast to the magnificent poodle, who now looked like a heavenly lady of the lake, glamorous and soaked.

You do often find great beauty hides in the strangest of places!

Freddie's Dungarees

YOU WILL NEED

- **One fat quarter of light to quilting weight 100% cotton fabric**
- **Four 10mm (⅜in) metal buttons**
- **Two press studs**
- **Contrast thread for topstitching**
- **Basic sewing kit (see Materials)**

Use a 0.5cm (¼in) seam allowance, unless a different amount is stated.

CUTTING OUT

1 Cut around your paper pattern pieces for the dungarees carefully using scissors. I cut on the black line, but to the outside not the inside.

2 Fold the fabric in half so that right sides are together. Pin your pattern pieces onto the fabric using **Fig.1** as a guide – note that the bib pocket and strap only need to be cut once, but they are shown here on two layers. Cut all pieces as stated on the pattern. Mark any triangles with a small snip to the centre. Mark pocket positions using tailor's tacks or a water-soluble pen.

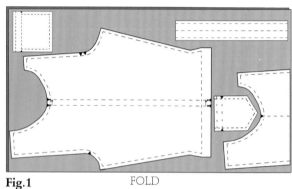

Fig.1   FOLD

MAKING UP

Sewing the Side Seams:

1 Working one main body piece at a time, press the fabric between the triangle and X notches into a fold, and make a pleat by taking the fold over to match the other triangle and dot notches (**Fig.2**). Press and pin in place.

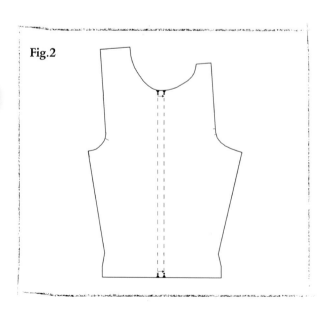

Fig.2

2 Edgestitch and then topstitch this fold to create an outer leg seam (**Fig.3**). The edgestitch should be 2mm (¹⁄₁₆in) away from the fold and the topstitch should be 4mm (³⁄₁₆in).

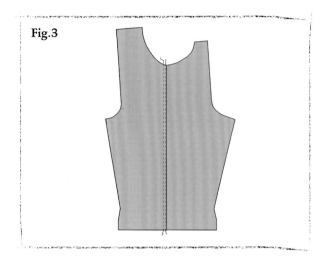

Fig.3

Making the Back Pockets:
1 Turn 0.5cm (¼in) on the top edge of the pocket to the wrong side and press. Then turn 1cm (⅜in) to the right side of the fabric and pin the edges in place. Sew 0.5cm (¼in) in on both edges (**Fig.4**).

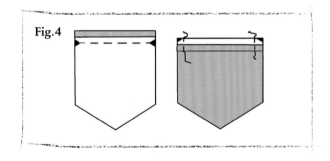

Fig.4

2 Trim excess seam allowance away at the corners of the fold. Turn through, pushing out the corners with a knitting needle. Turn and press the other edges of the pockets to the wrong side by 0.5cm (¼in) all the way around (**Fig.5**).

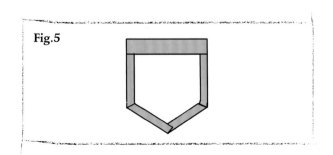

Fig.5

3 Edgestitch across the top of the pocket, stitching down to the point and then back up to create pocket profile stitch (**Fig.6**).

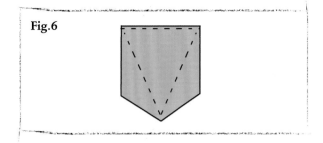

Fig.6

4 Position the pockets onto the leg panels and sew in place using an edgestitch. Leave the top edge free (**Fig.7**).

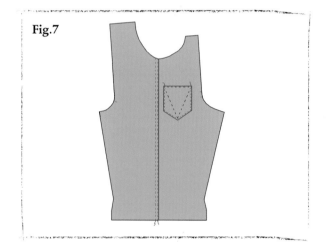

Fig.7

Sewing the Hems, Inside Leg Seams and Crotch:
1 Make the hems by turning 0.5cm (¼in) to the wrong side and then a further 0.5cm (¼in) to enclose the raw edges (**Fig.8**). Press and then edgestitch in place.

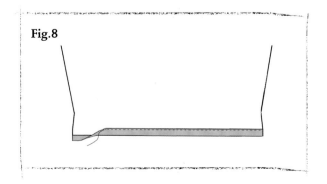

Fig.8

2 Working one leg at a time, with right sides together, match the inside leg seams and sew (**Fig.9**). Repeat for the other leg and press seams.

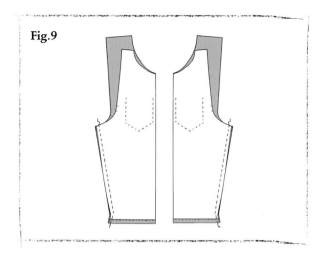

Fig.9

3 Turn one leg to be right side out and slide it, lower edge first, inside the other leg to sew the crotch. Matching edges and notches and inside leg seam, pin and sew the crotch (**Fig.10**).

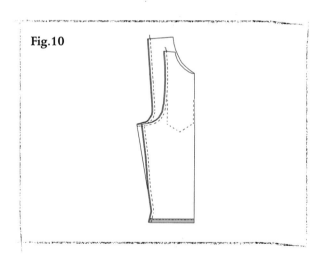

Fig.10

Making the Bib Pocket:
1 Turn 0.5cm (¼in) on the top edge of the pocket to the wrong side and press. Turn 1cm (⅜in) to the right side of the fabric and pin the edges in place. Sew 0.5cm (¼in) in on both edges (**Fig.11**).

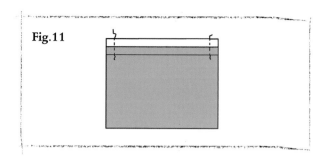

Fig.11

2 Trim excess seam allowance away at the corners of the fold. Turn through, pushing out the corners with a knitting needle. Turn and press the other edges of the pockets to the wrong side by 0.5cm (¼in) all the way around (**Fig.12**).

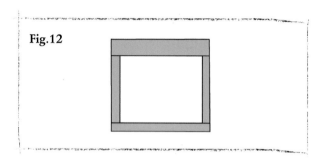

Fig.12

3 Topstitch along the top edge of the pocket about 8mm (⁵⁄₁₆in) from the top edge (**Fig.13**). Position the pocket onto the front bib and sew in place using an edgestitch. Leave the top edge free. Sew a pencil pocket 1cm (⅜in) in from the edge (**Fig.14**).

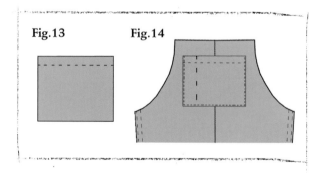

Fig.13   Fig.14

Making the Front Facing and Straps:
1 With right sides together, join centre front seams on front facing and then centre back seams, and then press open (**Fig.15**). Zigzag or overlock around lower edge of facing to finish.

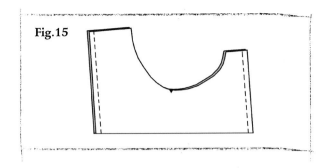

Fig.15

2 Use an iron to press in 0.5cm (¼in) on each long side of the strap and then press in half so that the folded edges meet (**Fig.16**). Open up the pressed pieces, refold each end so right sides are together and sew across ends. Trim the seam allowance, turn back through, push out the corners and then edgestitch down each side, about 2mm (¹⁄₁₆in) from the fold (**Fig.17**). Cut the strap in half (**Fig.18**).

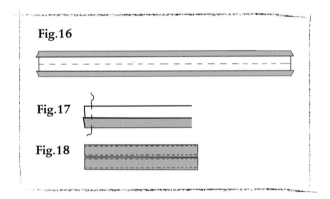

Fig.16

Fig.17

Fig.18

3 With right sides together, slip the facing over the dungarees, matching the corners. The notches on the sides of the facing will line up with the side seam on the dungarees. Pin and sew all the way around from the back around the curves of the side bodies, around the front bib, the other side and then up to the other side of the back, leaving the top of the back open (**Fig.19**).

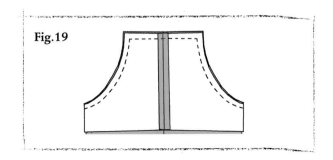

Fig.19

4 Insert the straps into the back, with the better side facing the right side of the dungarees and the raw edges of the straps going up into the open edge at the top of the back. Then sew across the back 0.5cm (¼in) down from the top back edge. Trim away the corners, and snip into the curves to allow the seams to sit flat when they are pressed (**Fig.20**).

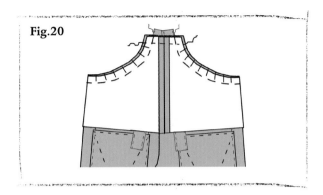

Fig.20

FINISHING OFF

1 Press the facing back inside the body of the dungarees, rolling the seams to the outside between your fingers and thumbs. Then edgestitch all the way around the top, about 2mm (¹⁄₁₆in) away from the edge.

2 Sew a metal button onto the top of each side seam. Sew a button onto each of the top corners on the front bib, position one side of a press stud under each button and sew in place. Then sew other half of each press stud onto each strap (**Fig.21**). It is worth putting the dungarees onto your badger to check the length of the straps before attaching – if they are too long, sew the press studs further up the straps.

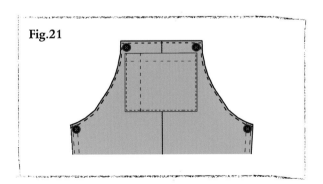

Fig.21

Freddie's Grandad Shirt

YOU WILL NEED

- **One fat quarter of striped light to quilting weight 100% cotton fabric**
- **Six 7mm (¼in) buttons**
- **Four press studs**
- **Basic sewing kit (see Materials)**

Use a 0.5cm (¼in) seam allowance, unless a different amount is stated.

CUTTING OUT

1 Cut around your paper pattern pieces for the grandad shirt carefully using scissors. I cut on the black line, but to the outside not the inside.

2 Fold the fabric in half so that right sides are together and so that stripes are running in line with fold. Pin your pattern pieces onto the fabric using **Fig.1** as a guide. Cut all pieces as stated on the pattern.

FOLD

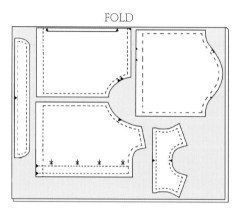

Fig.1

MAKING UP

Making the Front Plackets:

1 Take one shirt front and turn the front long edge to the wrong side by 0.5cm (¼in) and press (**Fig.2**). Turn a further 1cm (⅜in) to the wrong side and press (**Fig.3**). Repeat with second front, ensuring it is facing the other way. Edgestitch down each side of the placket (**Fig.4**).

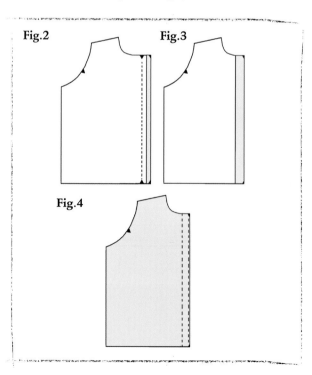

Fig.2 Fig.3

Fig.4

Making the Back Yoke:

1 Gather the top edge of the shirt back. Start and finish at the two outer notches (see Machine Sewing Techniques: Gathering) (**Fig.5** and **Fig.6**).

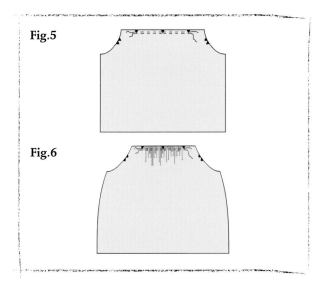

Fig.5

Fig.6

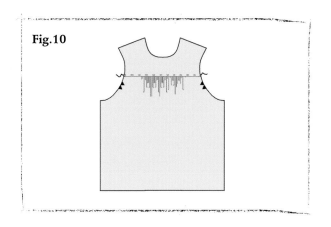

Fig.10

Making the Front Yoke:

1 Keeping the under yoke out of the way, take the front panels and match the front yoke seams to the front shoulders on each side. Pin in place and sew (**Fig.11**). The back will look like **Fig.12**.

2 Lay the back panel with right side facing upwards. Put one yoke on the top with right sides downwards. Match up yoke seams and pin. Adjust the gathering so that it fits to the space on the yoke, and so notches match (**Fig.7**). Flip the back over to the wrong side (**Fig.8**). Match up the remaining yoke and, with the right side facing downwards, pin in place through all the layers (remember to remove the original pins) (**Fig.9**).

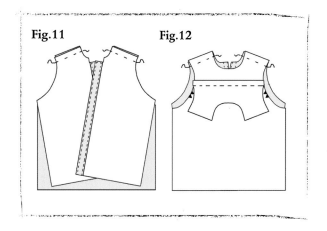

Fig.11   Fig.12

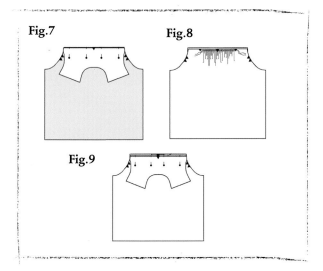

Fig.7   Fig.8

Fig.9

2 Press the seams towards the yoke. Press 0.5cm (¼in) seam allowance of free yoke to the wrong side and then lay it over the already sewn yoke, matching the folded edges to the sewing line, and slip stitch in place (**Fig.13**). Flip to the right side and edgestitch the front yokes through all layers (**Fig.14**).

3 Sew all layers together. Press the yokes back on themselves and then edgestitch the edge of the yoke through all layers (**Fig.10**).

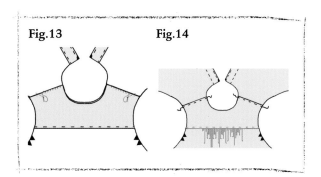

Fig.13   Fig.14

Sewing the Sleeve Hems:

1 Hem the sleeves by turning 0.5cm (¼in) to the wrong side and then a further 0.5cm (¼in). Press and then edgestitch through all layers (**Fig.15**).

Fig.15

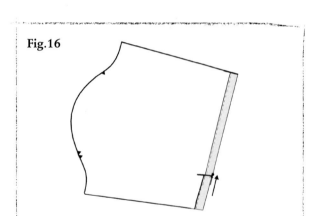

2 Use the pattern piece to mark the pleat positions. With the wrong side facing upwards bring the X to match the dot. Press and pin (**Fig.16**). Repeat with other sleeve, which will be a mirror image. Flip to be right side up and hand sew a button in place through the pleat layers to hold in place.

Fig.16

3 With right sides together, match one sleeve to the armhole using the notches to position. Pin in place and sew together (**Fig.17**). Repeat with the other sleeve and armhole. Press the seams towards the sleeve.

Fig.17

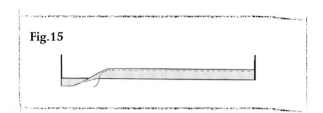

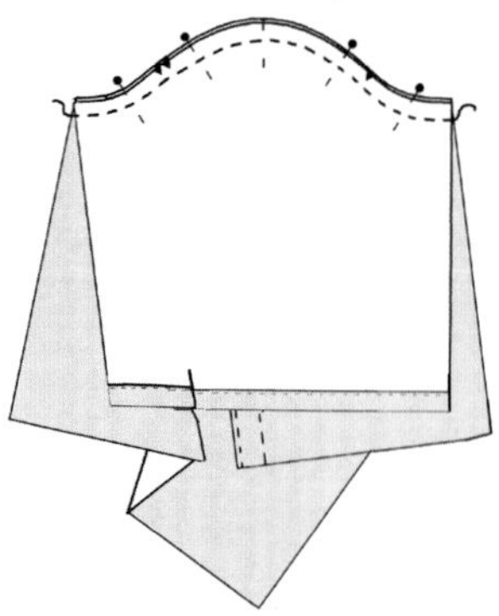

Making the Collar:

1 Staystitch 0.5cm (¼in) in from the edge of the neck, using a long stitch that can easily be removed. Snip into the fabric where the curves are tight on the neck but don't cut past the staystitching (**Fig.18**).

Fig.18

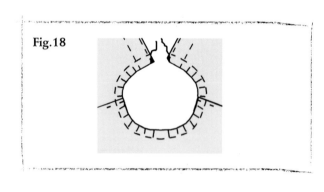

2 Take one collar piece and press the notched edge to the wrong side by 0.5cm (¼in) (**Fig.19**). With right sides together, pin the two collar pieces together, matching the corners, and sew along the two curved ends and the long un-notched edge. Note the pressed edge of one collar will mean it doesn't match up along the notched edge – see **Fig.20**. Trim the curves to reduce the bulk. Turn the collar out and push the curves out using a knitting needle or similar tool (**Fig.21**).

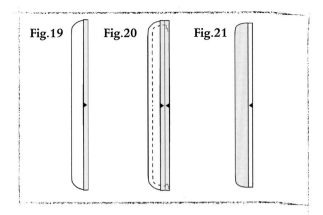

Fig.19 Fig.20 Fig.21

3 Pin the unturned collar piece into position on the right side of the shirt, using the centre back snip to guide you. The end of the collar will come right to the end of the plackets. Tack (baste) in place using a tiny seam allowance (slightly less than 0.5cm/¼in) then sew with a 0.5cm (¼in) seam allowance – you will need the snips in the neck edge to give the ease to enable you to sew in the collar strip (**Fig.22**).

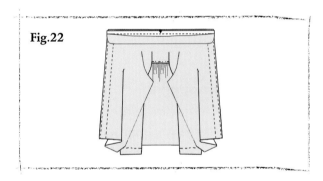

Fig.22

4 Using an iron, press the seam allowance away from the shirt and up towards the collar. Bring the free collar edge down to match your sewing line and enclose all the raw edges. Slip stitch the edge of the collar onto the line of stitching (see Hand Sewing Stitches: Slip Stitch) (**Fig.23**). Remove staystitching if visible and then edgestitch around the collar (**Fig.24**)

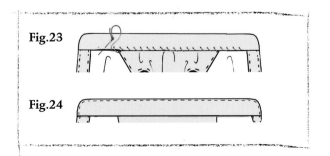

Fig.23

Fig.24

FINISHING OFF

1 With right sides together, match up the sleeve seams, underarm and side seams. Pin in place and sew (**Fig.25**). Press the seams towards the back of the shirt as far as you can.

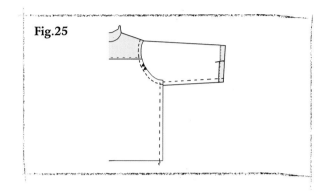

Fig.25

2 Hem the shirt by turning 0.5cm (¼in) to the wrong side and then a further 0.5cm (¼in). Press and edgestitch through all layers.

3 If you are not confident with making buttonholes you can just sew on your buttons and use press studs to fasten. Both methods are given here:

If making buttonholes, mark the button and buttonhole positions on the front using the pattern as a guide. Make buttonholes on the left-hand side (as worn). Cut through the buttonholes carefully using an unpicker and a pin at the far end of the buttonhole to ensure you don't rip any further than the buttonhole. Sew the buttons on the right-hand side through both the front and front facing (**Fig.26**).

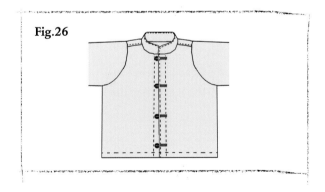

Fig.26

If using buttons with press studs, sew the buttons on left-hand side (as worn) through both the front and front facing. Position one side of a press stud under each button and sew in place. Sew the other half of each press stud onto the face of the right-hand side.

Freddie's Gilet

CUTTING OUT

1 Cut around your paper pattern pieces for the gilet carefully using scissors. I cut on the black line, but to the outside not the inside.

2 Fold the fabric in half so that right sides are together. Pin your pattern pieces onto the fabric using **Fig.1** as a guide. Cut all pieces as stated on the pattern. Mark any triangles with a small snip to the centre. Mark pocket positions using tailor's tacks or a water-soluble pen.

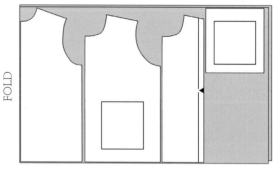

FOLD

Fig.1

3 Unpin your pattern pieces and cut the lining piece from the edge of the cotton fat quarter used for the Grandad Shirt.

YOU WILL NEED

- **20cm (8in) x 55cm (22in) 100% wool tweed for main fabric**
- **100% cotton striped fabric for the lining (from the same fat quarter as the Grandad Shirt)**
- **Eight 7mm (¼in) metal buttons**
- **Four press studs**
- **Contrast thread for topstitching**
- **Basic sewing kit (see Materials)**

Use a 0.5cm (¼in) seam allowance, unless a different amount is stated.

QUILTING DETAIL

This is an optional stage for adventurous and more experienced stitchers.

Using a contrasting coloured thread, topstitch the front and back pieces at a 45-degree angle to the centre front and centre back. Then repeat in the opposite direction at a 45-degree angle to make a diamond quilt pattern and trim all thread ends.

Make this easier by selecting a slightly longer stitch than usual and use the edge of your sewing foot to sew parallel to the first line that you made. You will find that the quilting can distort the fabric slightly but you will be able to press the shape back.

The pieces are shown without topstitching in the following diagrams.

MAKING UP

Making the Pockets:

1 Turn 1.5cm (⅝in) on the top edge of the pocket to the wrong side and press. At the top where the fabric is turned back, sew 1cm (⅜in) in on both edges. Trim the excess seam allowance away at the corners of the fold. Turn through, pushing out the corners with a knitting needle (**Fig.2**).

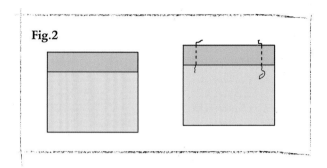

Fig.2

2 Turn and press the other edges of the pockets to the wrong side by 1cm (⅜in) all the way around (**Fig.3**). Sew across the pocket, 1cm (⅜in) down from the top (**Fig.4**). You need to use a 1cm (⅜in) seam allowance here because the tweed is too thick to turn back at 0.5cm (¼in).

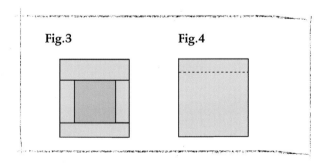

Fig.3   **Fig.4**

3 Position the pockets onto the front panels, using the pattern as a guide and sew onto the fronts using an edgestitch (see Machine Sewing Techniques: Edgestitch) (**Fig.5**).

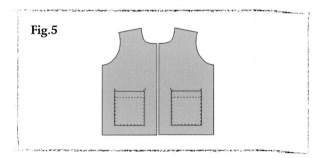

Fig.5

Sewing the Shoulders:

1 With right sides together, match the shoulder seam of one front to one back shoulder seam and sew. Repeat with the other front and the remaining back shoulder seam (**Fig.6**). Press seams open.

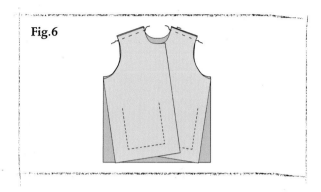

Fig.6

2 With right sides together, sew one front facing to one front lining, matching notches (**Fig.7**). Repeat with other front facing and other front lining. Press seams open (**Fig.8**).

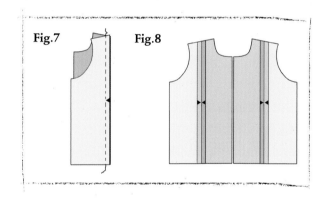

Fig.7   **Fig.8**

3 With right sides together, match the shoulder seam of one front lining to one back lining shoulder seam and sew. Repeat with the other front lining and the remaining back shoulder seam (**Fig.9**). Press seams open.

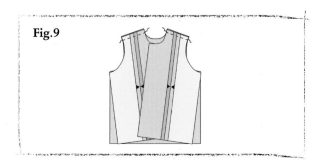

Fig.9

Sewing the Front Edges and Neckline:

1 With right sides together, match the edges of the lining up to the front hems, front edges and back neck. Pin in place and, starting at one side front, sew around the edge, finishing at the other side front. To pivot at a corner, leave your needle down in the fabric, lift the presser foot and swing the fabric to line up with the new angle (**Fig.10**).

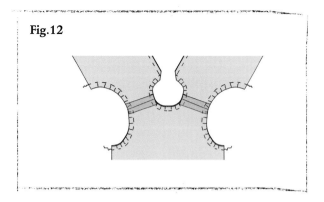

Fig.12

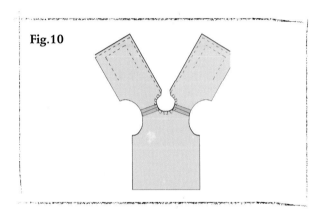

Fig.10

2 Trim excess seam allowances where there are points, and snip into the seam allowance through the neck curve to allow the seam allowance to sit flat once turned, but don't turn yet (**Fig.11**).

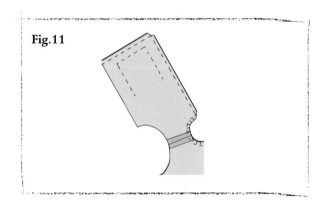

Fig.11

Sewing the Armholes and Side Seams:

1 Pin the lining to the main fabric around each armhole, matching the shoulder seams and edges. Sew each armhole. Snip into the seam allowance on the armholes to allow the seam to sit flat once turned (**Fig.12**).

2 Push each front through the opening of the shoulder seam to the back and turn through (**Fig.13**). Use a knitting needle to push out the points and corners. Roll the edges between your fingers and thumb to get the seams on the edge and press the gilet flat (**Fig.14**).

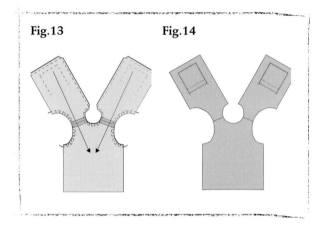

Fig.13   Fig.14

3 With right sides together, match the side seams of the outer fabric with the lining, ensuring that the armhole seams match. The front piece will be enclosed between the back outer fabric and the back lining. You will notice that the back edges are 1cm (⅜in) longer than the front, because the front hem is already turned up and there is a little more to turn up on the back hem. Pin in place and sew, from the armhole down to the hem (**Fig.15**).

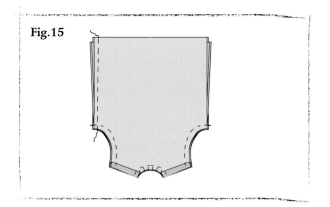

Fig.15

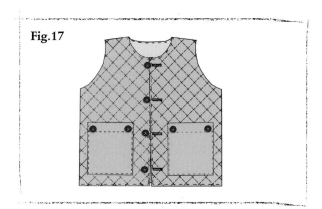

Fig.17

FINISHING OFF

1 Turn the gilet out and press the side seam flat. Turn the back outer and lining hem edges up by 1cm (⅜in) and slip stitch together to enclose the raw edges (see Hand Sewing Stitches: Slip Stitch). Edgestitch around the hem, the front edges, neckline and back down the front to finish at the hem (**Fig.16**).

Fig.16

2 If you are not confident with making buttonholes you can just sew on your buttons and use press studs to fasten. Both methods are given here:

If making buttonholes, mark the button and buttonhole positions on the front using the pattern as a guide. Make buttonholes on the left-hand side (as worn). Cut through the buttonholes carefully using an unpicker and a pin at the far end of the buttonhole to ensure you don't rip any further than the buttonhole. Sew the buttons on the right-hand side through both the front and front facing (**Fig.17**).

If using buttons with press studs, sew the buttons on left-hand side (as worn) through both the front and front facing. Position one side of a press stud under each button and sew in place. Sew the other half of each press stud onto the face of the right-hand side.

3 To finish, sew two buttons onto the top edges of each pocket (**Fig.17**).

Luna GETS lost

The morning was bright and Luna couldn't wait to see what Freddie and Reynard had planned for the day. What was meant to be a photo shoot trip had turned into the most brilliant of holidays.

Everyone else had left and Luna was glad to be in the company of two wonderful friends. A little time away was just what she needed. Reynard seemed to be refreshed in the country air and Luna loved to take a break from the city and remember what it feels like to get your paws dirty. Freddie was grateful for the help too; a farmer's work is never done. Luna put the kettle on to boil and looked around Freddie's kitchen. "I wonder where everyone is!" our favourite rabbit thought. Reynard would still be in bed, she was pretty sure of that. As for Freddie, he was probably in the yard, working hard or singing to his seedlings.

Luna wandered outside, neatening the bow on her brand new dress as she did. Freddie had been kind enough to lend her his great-great grandmother's sewing machine – he had dug it up from the cellar complete with a pile of marvellous fabrics. They had all sat one night as she sewed and told scary stories of hunters and butchers.

Luna couldn't help but skip as she searched the farmyard for Freddie. His tractor was there. And the hens had all been fed. On the very edge of the farm there was a woodland, a twisty path leading from the dry-stone walls deep within. Even on this perfect crisp morning it looked ominous. " I wonder," thought Luna, "Freddie has mentioned he likes to pick mushrooms." And with a nervous sigh our brave little bunny set off.

Luna walked and walked and walked. The path grew narrower and the sky seemed to be getting further away. A few drops of rain started to fall and one of them hit Luna square on her brown twitchy nose. "Oh, please, oh please don't rain!" Luna began to run.

Freddie and Reynard sat eating crumpets whilst looking out of the kitchen window. What had been a fine morning had quickly turned. Huge plops of rain formed streams outside.

"Where on this fine earth is Luna Lapin? I'm awful worried," said Reynard, who, by this point had taken to pacing. "And I," replied Freddie, getting up quickly to pull on his coat. "You stay here, she will be soaked through. Make sure the fire is hot and the kettle is boiled." And without another word he marched out the door.

Luna ran as fast as her legs could carry her. Eventually she came to a hollowed-out tree that provided her with shelter; the stories of hunters from the night before howled with the wind through her head. Every creak and crack was a threat. Luna sat snuggled up in a little ball sobbing, wishing that one of her friends would find her. Eventually our usually lion-hearted rabbit fell asleep, covered in leaves from the forest floor, cold and wet.

Luna woke with a jump. Her ears pricked, there it was again. Crack, crack, crack. Daring herself to peek, Luna opened her left eye. What was that! Something shiny, densely black, the pearls of rainwater resting and rolling from its surface. Luna opened another eye. It was a welly! And not just any welly, Freddie's welly! The most perfect welly Luna had ever seen. He had found her! She could almost kiss him.

"Come on you, let's get you home."

Luna's Tie Shoulder Dress

CUTTING OUT

1 Cut around your paper pattern pieces for the tie shoulder dress carefully using scissors. I like to cut on the black line, but to the outside not the inside.

2 You will need to make two folds in your fat quarter so that the edges meet in the middle with right sides of the fabric facing out. Pin your pattern pieces onto the fabric using **Fig.1** as a guide. Cut all pieces as stated on the pattern. Mark any triangles with a small snip to the centre.

FOLD

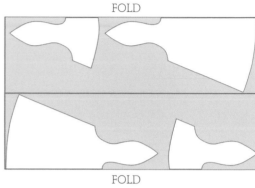

FOLD

Fig.1

MAKING UP

Sewing the Facings to the Dress:
1 With right sides together, match one facing piece to one body piece, pinning around what look like bunny ears. Sew in place taking your time around the curves. Where you reach the corner at the top, leave your needle down in the fabric, lift the presser foot, pivot to change direction, lower the presser foot again and continue sewing (**Fig.2**). Repeat with the remaining facing and body piece.

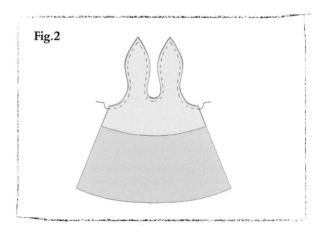

Fig.2

YOU WILL NEED

- **One fat quarter of fine cotton with a non-directional print**
- **60cm (23½in) of 1.5cm (⅝in) wide cotton lace for hem (optional)**
- **Basic sewing kit (see Materials)**

Use a 0.5cm (¼in) seam allowance, unless a different amount is stated.

2 Trim the seam allowances at the points and clip the seam allowances around the curves to allow for turning through (**Fig.3**).

38

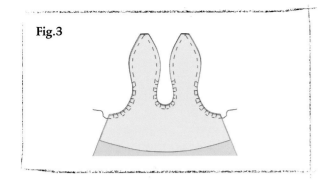

Fig.3

3 Turn through to the right side pushing out the points with the closed end of your scissors or a knitting needle/chopstick. Roll the seams out to be on the edge and press flat with an iron (**Fig.4**).

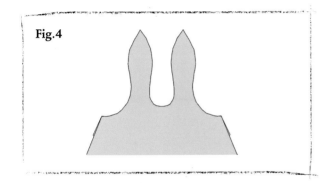

Fig.4

Sewing the Side Seams:
1 Open up the facings away from the main body so that the shoulder ties fold back and sit on the main body of the dress (**Fig.5**).

2 With right sides touching, place the two dress pieces together matching the side seams of the body pieces and the facings to one another. Pin and sew in place making sure the armhole seams are level. (**Fig.6**).

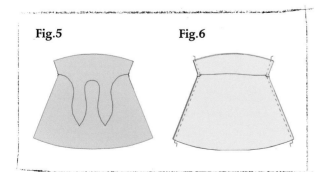

Fig.5   **Fig.6**

3 Press the seam allowances open and finish the lower edge of the neck facing with zigzag stitch (or an overlocker if you have one) to neaten the raw edges.

4 Slip stitch the facings down onto the side seams loosely to hold in place (see Hand Sewing Stitches: Slip Stitch).

Sewing the Hem:
1 Neaten the hem with a zigzag stitch (or overlocker if you have one) and then press up to the wrong side by 1cm (⅜in) (**Fig.7**).

2 If you are attaching some lace to the hem, pin in place 0.5cm (¼in) onto the turned hem with a 1cm (⅜in) overlap at one side seam. Sew all the way around the hem 0.25cm (⅛in) up from finished fabric hem working on the right side of the fabric (**Fig.8**).

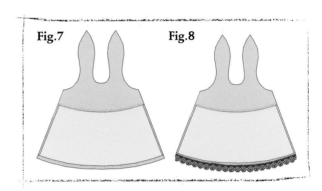

Fig.7   **Fig.8**

FINISHING OFF

1 Tie one set of straps loosely with a single knot and then tie another knot using a reef knot method (right over left for first knot, then left over right for second knot) to pull tight and flat. Pop the dress onto Luna and tie the other set of straps in the same manner. Pull tight to maximise the bunny ear ends. **Fig.9** is a view from above.

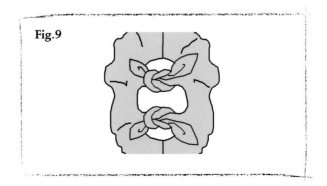

Fig.9

Wellies

YOU WILL NEED

- **15cm (6in) x 48cm (19in) black felt**
- **Two buckles with an inner width of about 0.5cm (¼in)**
- **4cm (1½in) of 1.6cm (⅝in) wide grosgrain ribbon**
- **Contrast thread for topstitching**
- **Basic sewing kit (see Materials)**

Use a 0.5cm (¼in) seam allowance, unless a different amount is stated.

CUTTING OUT

1 Cut around your paper pattern pieces for the wellies carefully using scissors. I like to cut on the black line, but to the outside not the inside.

2 Fold the felt in half and pin on your pattern pieces using **Fig.1** as a guide. Cut all pieces as stated on the pattern. Mark any triangles with a small snip to the centre. On ONLY one pair of boots cut down the marked line. The boots side with the cut line are now the outer pieces.

FOLD

Fig.1

MAKING UP

Sewing the Front Seam:

1 Match one outer boot to one inner boot piece and sew along the curved front edge. Repeat with other outer and inner but remember through the whole process you need to make two boots that mirror one another. Snip into the tight ankle curve (**Fig.2**).

2 Trim two pieces of grosgrain ribbon to be 1.5cm (⅝in) deep and using the width of the ribbon.

3 Fold the cut edges back on themselves so that the folded piece measures 8mm (⁵⁄₁₆in) by the full width of the ribbon (**Fig.3**).

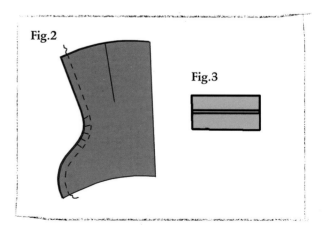

Fig.2

Fig.3

4 With the boots right side out, position the tab over the front seam of each boot so that the top folded edge of the ribbon is 1cm (⅜in) down from the top edge of the boot. Zigzag stitch all the way around the tab (**Fig.4**).

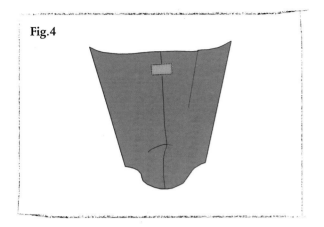

Fig.4

Making the Side Gusset and Attaching the Straps:

1 Take the rectangular side gusset and position it under the cut on the outer boot. Open up the outer boot top edge so that the top edges are 1.5cm (⅝in) apart with the side gusset underneath.

2 Pin in place – in this picture we have made the top layer transparent so you can see the position of the side gusset underneath (**Fig.5**).

3 Edgestitch down both sides of each strap (see Machine Sewing Techniques: Edgestitch).

4 Take one strap and push one of the short ends between the front outer and the side gusset – so that top edge of strap is 1.5cm (⅝in) down from upper edge of boot. Edgestitch all the way around the V shape – making sure you keep the other end of the strap free. Repeat with the other boot (**Fig.6**).

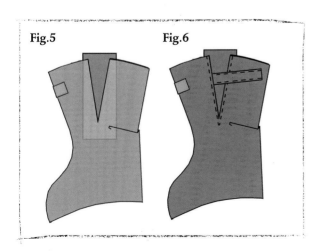

Fig.5   Fig.6

Sewing on the Buckles:

1 Trim the strap to measure 3cm (1¼in) long. Thread the buckle onto the strap and push the prong through the strap about 1cm (⅜in) away from the sewn edge that is caught into the gusset/boot. Take the free end of the strap, thread back through the buckle and tack (baste) in place along the back edge of the boot so that the strap is sitting parallel to top edge of boot. Trim away the excess of the side gusset to line up with top of boot. Repeat with other boot and buckle (**Fig.7**).

Sewing the Back Seams:

1 Refold the boot so that the inner and outer are right sides together, match the back edges and sew down the back. You can trim away the extra felt around the side gusset if you want. Repeat with other boot (**Fig.8**).

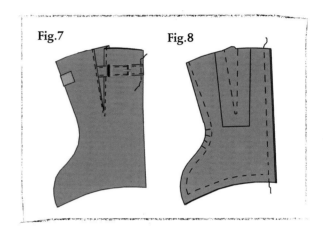

Fig.7   Fig.8

Sewing the Sole to the Boot:

1 With right sides together, match the boot seams to the sole notches (the wide end of the sole is toe end), tack (baste) the sole onto the boot, easing the felt in as necessary and sew (**Fig.9**).

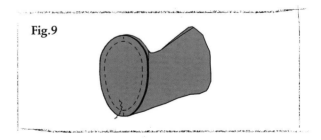

Fig.9

FINISHING OFF

Turn the boots through. You will be able to push the wellies onto the leg and foot of your animal, but you may have to manipulate them a bit. If you want to tuck dungarees into the wellies you may have to push them down into the wellies using a knitting needle.

Luna GOES TO THE Seaside

Winnie and Luna had always been friends, ever since they were small. They spent many a summer counting clouds and making daisy chains.

Wilhelmina was her born name and she was a wood mouse. I'm not sure what you know about wood mice, but she was exactly as you would expect – she had beady black eyes and a shiny little nose. Her whiskers stood on end when she was scared, or amazed, or just for any reason at all. Winnie was a timid little thing.

Luna loved her very much; she had many fond memories of playing down-on-one knee or French cricket with her and Alfie. Luna laughed to herself. She was so excited to be going to see her sweet old friend.

A clatter of cogs, swirling smoke and the tang of burning coal signalled the start of the journey. Luna picked up her suitcase, a lovely brown thing, slightly battered and splattered with the memories of travels past, and hopped aboard, her anticipation building with every chug of the big engine. When the train tracks started to hug the coastline, Luna knew her destination was near and she eagerly drank in the views, especially as they travelled over the viaduct at the bay of Whitesands.

Luna's train pulled in to the sleepy little station, the red pillars bright against the Victorian sandstone, the green of the roof shimmering in the mid-morning light. Luna breathed in sharply. She could smell the seaside, the salt and smog of the train mixing to create the most wonderful perfume. A little paw was waving at her from the platform – Winnie was always dressed so wonderfully, almost as if she was from another time. She wore a dress so beautiful Luna couldn't help but get a little green. The check fabric was simple, weaving together reds and navy blues on a perfect dove grey. The dress wrapped to the side and its skirt rippled with the slowing train.

Winnie looked like a scene from Casablanca or some other famous film filled with mystery and charm. The little animals ran to each other exclaiming in glee, chattering happily in the way good friends who have missed each other do.

Luna and Winnie had decided to spend the day doing everything typically seaside. They would eat ice cream, walk along the promenade, ride a donkey and paddle in the sea if the weather was kind.

The happy pair walked all the way down to the Lido. It was unused, overgrown and still as beautiful as the pictures that they put on the postcards of this little seaside town. It was not beautiful in a glorious way but in the abandoned kind of beauty that comes with sadness of a once loved place. The girls stood and pondered how wonderful this place must have been all those years ago, when children splashed and ladies stood and talked, and gentlemen gathered on benches. When the plants only grew where they should have grown. When the café was filled with lemonade and teacakes. Winnie told Luna how much she loved this place, how much she longed for it's restoration so that she may one day bring her own babies here to play. Luna listened intently and her mind began to whirl.

"I think I can help," the rabbit with her big floppy ears whispered. And Luna had quite the idea. She would gather her friends in high places, they would place the Lido centre fold of the magazine, she would draw in all the possibilities: Reynard would write something to make hearts sing, Clem would bring the people, and Mae would bring the glamour. Alfie could play music, and Freddie, well, Freddie would be there to help anyone that ever needed help, just as he always did. They would make this little town everything it was on paper, and the people, they would come.

Wilhelmina's Wrap Dress

CUTTING OUT

1 Cut around your paper pattern pieces for the wrap dress carefully using scissors. I like to cut on the black line, but to the outside not the inside.

2 Fold the fabric in half with right sides together. If you are using a check fabric be aware of matching the long lower pattern edges up with the fabric pattern so the finished garment looks balanced. Pin your pattern pieces onto the fabric using **Fig.1** as a guide. Remember the pocket goes on the bias. Cut all pieces as stated on the pattern. Mark any triangles with a small snip to the centre – noting where there is an 'on the fold' snip. Mark any pocket positions using tailor's tacks or a water-soluble pen.

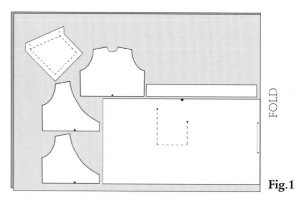

FOLD

Fig.1

YOU WILL NEED

- **35cm (13¾in) x 110cm (43¼in) light to mid weight linen or linen look print fabric**
- **One press stud**
- **Basic sewing kit (see Materials)**

Use a 0.5cm (¼in) seam allowance, unless a different amount is stated.

MAKING UP

Making the Ties:
1 Press in both long edges of the tie by 0.5cm (¼in) (**Fig.2**).

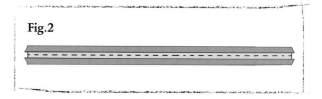

Fig.2

2 Then press the strip in half so the raw edges are enclosed and edgestitch along the long open edges (see Machine Sewing Techniques: Edgestitch) (**Fig.3**). Repeat to make the second tie.

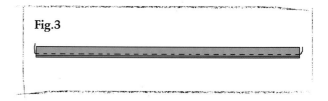

Fig.3

Making the Pockets:

1 Using your snips as a guide, turn 1.5cm (⅝in) along the top edge of the pocket to the wrong side and press. Secure each short folded-back edge with a short row of machine sewing 1cm (⅜in) in from both edges (**Fig.4**).

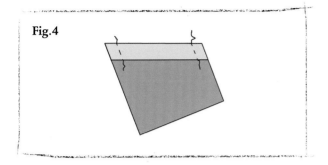

Fig.4

2 Trim off seam allowances at corners. Turn the folded section through to the right side, pushing out the corners with a knitting needle.

3 Turn and press the other three edges of the pockets to the wrong side by 1cm (⅜in).

4 Sew across the hem along the top of the pocket 1cm (⅜in) down from the folded edge (**Fig.5**).

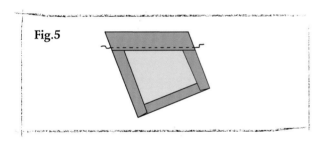

Fig.5

Sewing the Pockets to the Skirt of the Dress:

1 Position the pockets onto the skirt panels, using your markings as a guide and sew the pockets onto the skirt using an edgestitch (**Fig.6**).

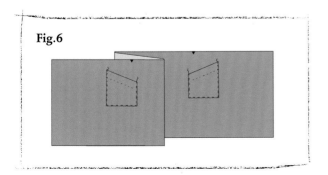

Fig.6

Sewing the Shoulder Seams in the Outer and the Lining of the Bodice:

1 With right sides together, match the shoulder of one outer front to one outer back shoulder and sew together.

2 Repeat with the other front and the remaining back shoulder and press the seams open (**Fig.7**).

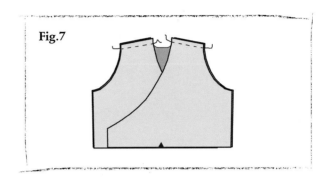

Fig.7

3 Repeat with the lining pieces.

Sewing the Outer and Lining Bodices Together:

1 With right sides touching, place the outer and lining together. Match the edges of the lining up to the outer around the front and back neck. Pin in place and starting at one side front, sew all around the neck edge (**Fig.8**).

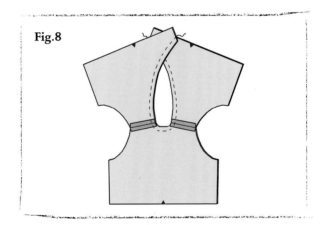

Fig.8

2 Snip into the seam allowance along the neck curve to allow the seam allowance to sit flat once turned.

3 Still with right sides together, pin the lining to the outer around each armhole, matching the shoulder seams and edges and sew around each armhole (**Fig.9**).

4 Snip into the seam allowance along the armholes to allow the seam to sit flat once turned.

5 Push each front through the opening of the shoulder seam to the back to turn right side out (**Fig.10**).

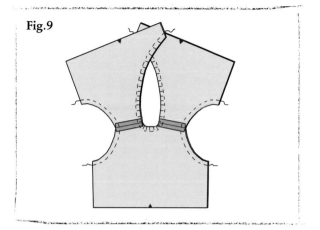

Fig.9

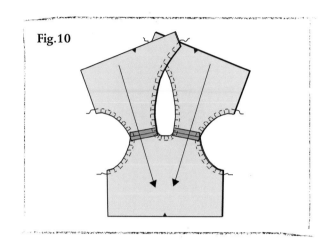

Fig.10

6 Roll the edges between your fingers and thumb to get the seams on the edge and press bodice flat.

7 On the left-hand side as worn, pin a tie so that it is 1cm (⅜in) up from the lower edge of the bodice. Pin in place so the long end is trailing inside the bodice (**Fig.11**).

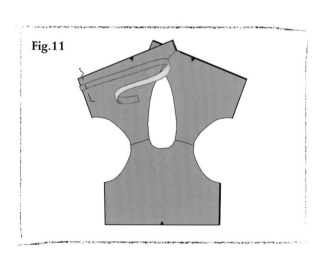

Fig.11

Sewing the Bodice Side Seams:

1 Working one side at a time and with right sides together, match and pin one front side seam to one back side seam (of the outer only), open out the lining and continue across the armhole seam onto the front and back linings. Make sure that the armhole seams match. Sew this side seam and repeat with the other side seam (**Fig.12**).

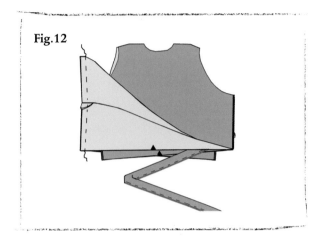

Fig.12

Sewing the Skirt:

1 To make the hem turn up 0.5cm (¼in) to the wrong side and press, then turn up a further 1cm (⅜in) and sew in place.

2 Repeat along the short ends of the skirt (**Fig.13**).

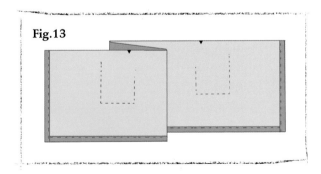

Fig.13

3 Gather the un-hemmed upper edge of the skirt (see Machine Sewing Techniques: Gathering). Draw up the gathers until the upper edge of the skirt measures roughly 35cm (13¾in) (**Fig.14**).

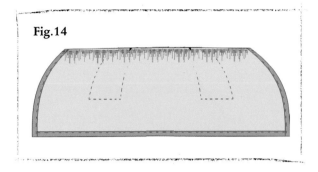

Fig.14

Sewing the Skirt to the Bodice:

1 With right sides together, match the gathered top of the skirt to the lower edge of the outer bodice only. Position each end of the skirt 0.5cm (¼in) in from the edge of the bodice on each side as the bodice still has to be finished. Adjust your gathers to be evenly spread so that the notches on the skirt correspond to the side seams on the bodice and keep the bodice lining out of the way. Sew the two layers together with the gathers facing upwards (**Fig.15**).

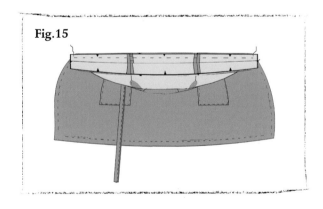

Fig.15

2 Remove any visible gathering threads and press the skirt seam allowance up towards the bodice.

FINISHING OFF

1 To finish the short ends of the bodice, turn the bodice fronts so they are right sides together again and on the right-hand side as worn, pin a tie in between the outer and lining layers, so that it is wedged up against the already stitched neck seam of the bodice, and pin in place so the long end is trailing inside the bodice. Sew in place (**Fig.16**).

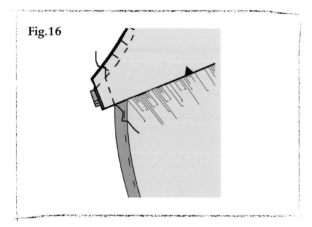

Fig.16

2 Trim off any excess seam allowance at the corners and turn through, pushing the corners out.

3 To finish off the bodice lining, fold up the 1cm (⅜in) seam allowance along the lower edge of the lining to the wrong side and match and pin to the seamline on the skirt.

4 Slip stitch in place by hand to enclose all raw edges (see Hand Sewing Stitches: Slip Stitch).

5 Position one side of the press stud on the left front short edge and then sew the other half onto the right front bodice lining (**Fig.17**).

Fig.17

Wilhelmina's Pintuck Top

YOU WILL NEED

- **60cm (23½in) x 30cm (11¾in) linen or linen blend fabric**
- **1m (39in) of 1cm (⅜in) wide lace (optional)**
- **Two 7mm (¼in) buttons**
- **Two press studs**
- **Basic sewing kit (see Materials)**

Use a 0.5cm (¼in) seam allowance, unless a different amount is stated.

CUTTING OUT

1 Cut around your paper pattern pieces for the pintuck top carefully using scissors. I like to cut on the black line, but to the outside not the inside.

2 Fold the fabric in half with right sides together. Pin your pattern pieces onto the fabric using **Fig.1** as a guide. Cut all pieces as stated on the pattern. Mark any triangles with a small snip to the centre – noting where there is an 'on the fold' snip. Mark pintuck positions using tailor's tacks or a water-soluble pen.

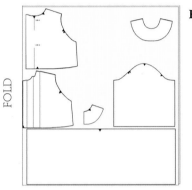

Fig.1

MAKING UP

Sewing the Pintucks on the Front:

1 With wrong sides together, press along each marked foldline for the pintucks and sew about 0.25cm (⅛in) in from the fold. Press each set of pintucks so that they face away from each other and lay towards each side seam (**Fig.2**).

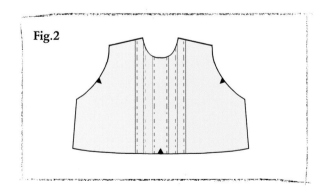

Fig.2

Sewing the Shoulder Seams:

1 With right sides together, match the shoulder of one back to one front shoulder and sew. Repeat with the other back and the remaining front shoulder. Press seams open (**Fig.3**).

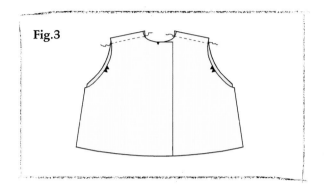

Fig.3

Making and Attaching the Neck Facing:

1 With right sides together, match the shoulder of one back facing to one front facing shoulder and sew. Repeat with the other back facing shoulder and the remaining front facing shoulder (**Fig.4**).

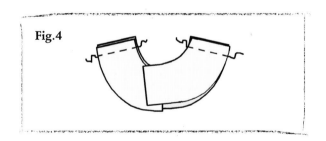

Fig.4

2 Press the seams open and finish the lower curved edge of the neck facing with zigzag stitch (or an overlocker if you have one) to finish the raw edges.

3 Place the neck facing onto the neck of the top with right sides together. Match and pin the short back edges of the facings to the upper back edges of the blouse and sew (be aware that the facing will look smaller than the neck of the blouse at this stage, don't worry!) (**Fig.5**).

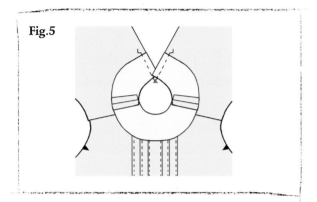

Fig.5

4 Match up the shoulder seams in the neck and facing. To get them to match you will need to fold the centre back edge back on itself with right sides touching using the notch on the centre back as a fold point. Pin around the neck edges, and then sew (**Fig.6**).

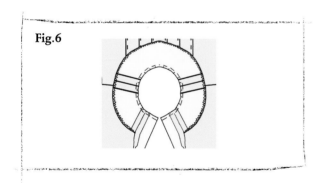

Fig.6

5 Trim the seam allowance back to 0.25cm (⅛in), snipping into the edge of the seam allowance in the curved parts to allow for turning through (**Fig.7**). Press the remainder of the centre back edges 0.5cm (¼in) to the wrong side.

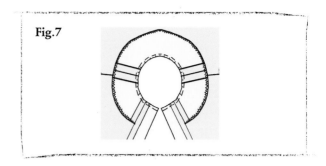

Fig.7

6 Turn the facing through to the right side pushing the corners out with your knitting needle. Roll the seam out to be on the edge and press flat with an iron (**Fig.8**). Turn and press the back edges below the facing to the wrong side by 1cm (⅜in).

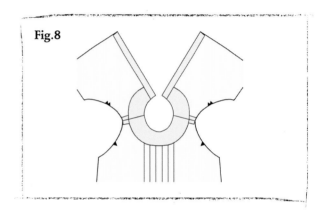

Fig.8

Making and Attaching the Sleeves:

1 Hem the sleeves by turning 0.5cm (¼in) to the wrong side and then a further 0.5cm (¼in). Press in place and sew through all the layers (**Fig.9**).

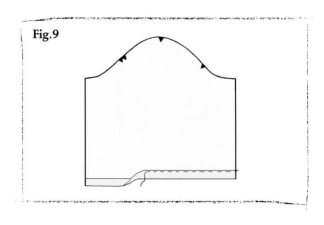

Fig.9

2 With right sides together, match one sleeve to an armhole using the notches to position and to ensure you have the correct sleeve in the correct armhole. Pin in place and sew (**Fig.10**).

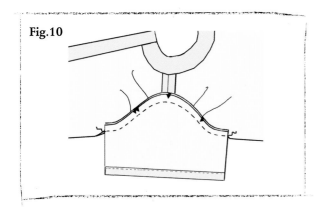

Fig.10

3 Repeat with the the other sleeve and armhole. Press seams towards body.

Making and Attaching the Lower Skirt Frills:

1 Make the hems on the lower skirt frills by turning 0.5cm (¼in) to the wrong side, then a further 1cm (⅜in) to enclose the raw edges. Press in place and sew through all the layers (**Fig.11**).

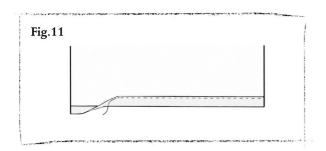

Fig.11

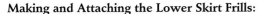

2 Attach the optional lace at this point. Pin it in place so that it sits approx. 0.25cm (⅛in) onto the wrong side of the hem. Tack (baste) in place first, then using an edgestitch sew in place with a machine (see Machine Sewing Techniques: Edgestitch). Alternatively you can sew it in place with an invisible hand stitch.

3 Gather along the top un-hemmed edge of the lower skirt frills. Don't secure the ends of your gathering at this stage (see Machine Sewing Techniques: Gathering) (**Fig.12** and **Fig.13**).

Fig.12

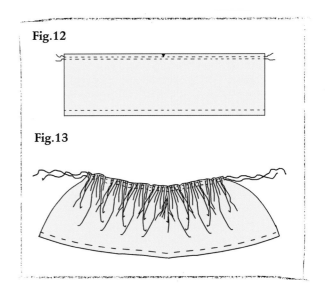

Fig.13

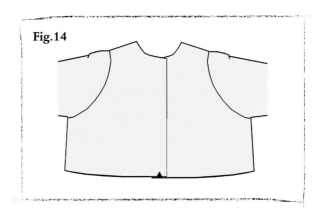

4 Overlap the back bodice edges so that the notches line up and so that the left-hand side as worn is over the top of the right-hand side as worn. Tack (baste) in place (**Fig.14**).

Fig.14

5 With right sides together, match the gathered top of one of the lower skirts to the lower edge of the front bodice. Adjust your gathers to be evenly spread so that the notches match. Sew through all the layers. Remove any visible gathering threads and press the seam allowance upwards. Repeat this step with the back bodice and the other lower skirt (**Fig.15**).

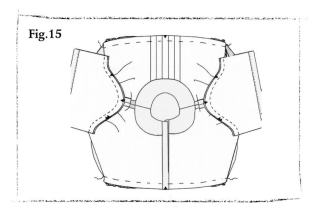

Fig.15

Sewing the Underarm and Side Seams of the Bodice:

1 With right sides together, pin the underarm and side seams together taking care to match up the armhole seams and sew. Press seams towards the back of the top as far as you can. Snip the fabric once at the underarm and turn the top inside out (**Fig.16**).

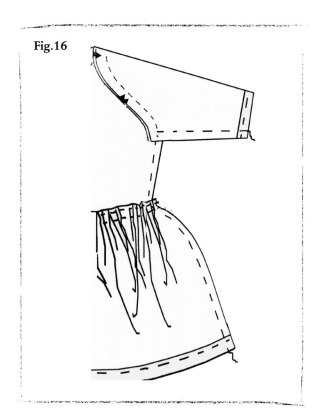

Fig.16

Sewing the Optional Neck Lace Trim:

1 Measure the length of the neck and add 2cm (¾in) to the measurement. Cut the lace to this measurement.

2 Pin the lace so that it sits approx. 0.25cm (⅛in) onto the wrong side of the neckline and turn back 1cm (⅜in) of the lace at each end of the neck opening. Tack (baste) in place first, then using an edgestitch sew in place with a machine (see Machine Sewing Techniques: Edgestitch) (**Fig.17**). Alternatively you can sew it in place with an invisible hand stitch.

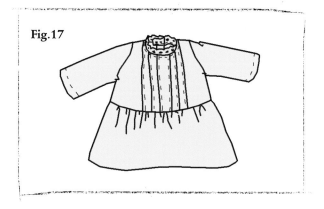

Fig.17

FINISHING OFF

1 Mark button positions on the left-hand side of the back of the bodice as worn, using the pattern as a guide and sew your buttons in place.

2 Position one side of a press stud under each button and sew in place. Then sew the other half of each press stud onto the face of the right-hand side as worn.

Suitcase

YOU WILL NEED

- **50cm (19¾in) x 25cm (10in) of faux leather**
- **50cm (19¾in) x 25cm (10in) double-sided heavy weight iron-on interfacing**
- **50cm (19¾in) x 25cm (10in) cotton lining**
- **Two 1cm (⅜in) wide D rings with base attachment or simple D rings**
- **Flexible fabric glue such as Fabritac**
- **Strong needle**
- **Tonal thread (a couple of shades lighter than the fabric to create a contrast)**
- **Basic sewing kit (see Materials)**

CUTTING OUT

1 Cut around your paper pattern pieces for the suitcase carefully using scissors. I like to cut on the black line, but to the outside not the inside.

2 On your fabric, draw around your pattern pieces to avoid pinning – this will minimise puncture marks being visible on the finished project. Use **Fig.1** as a guide. Mark the corner dots shown on the pattern with a water-soluble pen or similar. Cut into the notches on the lid. Unpin your pattern pieces and recut on the lining and interfacing. IMPORTANT: There is 0.5cm (¼in) difference between the base and the lid – which means you might muddle the pieces up – so find a way of differentiating.

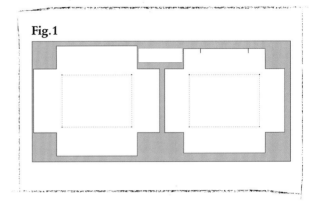

Fig.1

MAKING UP

Making the Layers of the Base and Lid:

1 Trim 1cm (⅜in) from the edges of the interfacing and the lining along the four long edges on the lid and base panels. Lay the fabric wrong side up, then the interfacing, then the lining right side up. Use a warm to hot iron on the lining side to press and fuse the layers together. You might find the glue on the interfacing only really sticks when the fabric has cooled (**Fig.2** and **Fig.3**).

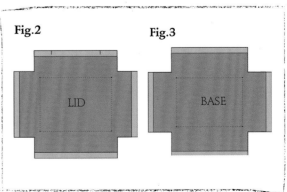

Fig.2 LID   **Fig.3** BASE

2 Identify the edge on the lid which is the extension edge – this has two notches in it. The area between the notches should not be glued. Use fabric glue on all other edges which have no lining or interfacing on them on the lid and base. Allow the glue to become tacky before pressing the outer edges down onto the lining by 1cm (⅜in) all the way around. Use a heavy book or Wonderclips to hold in place until the glue is dry (**Fig.4** and **Fig.5**).

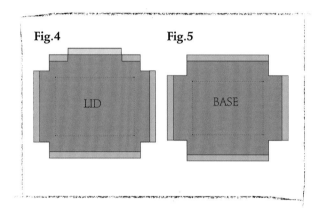

Fig.4   Fig.5

LID   BASE

3 Take the bag handle and apply glue to the wrong side of the fabric. Allow the glue to become tacky and fold the two long edges in to meet one another. Weight or use Wonderclips to hold in place until the glue is dry (**Fig.6** and **Fig.7**).

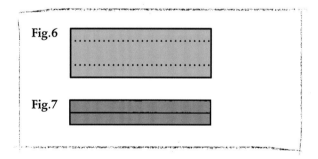

Fig.6

Fig.7

Sewing the Edges of the Base and Lid:

1 With wrong sides to the inside and using the marked spots as your guide, finger-fold the base fabric between the spots. Edgestitch (see Machine Sewing Techniques: Edgestitch) between the spots on each edge about 2mm (⅟₁₆in) from the fold, one side at a time – reversing a couple of stitches at the beginning and end of each stitching line (**Fig.8**, **Fig.9** and **Fig.10**).

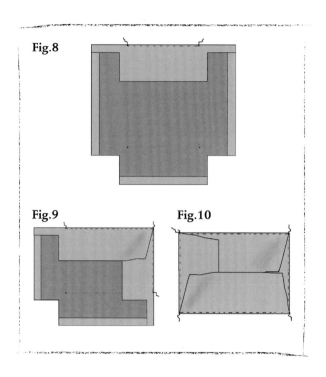

Fig.8

Fig.9   Fig.10

2 Repeat with lid. Trim any threads.

Sewing the Corners of the Base:

1 Working one corner at a time with right sides together, match the seam allowances making sure the folded edges match. Start at the folded edges, a little way in, and reverse back to the edge and then come forward, using a 1.2cm (½in) seam allowance. Sew just inside the marked spot and fasten off securely (**Fig.11** and **Fig.12**).

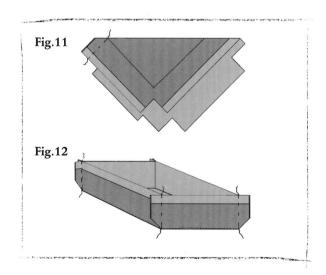

Fig.11

Fig.12

2 Trim the seam allowances back to a scant 0.25cm (⅛in).

Sewing the Corners of the Lid:

1 Sew the corners of the lid as you did for the base, but this time use a 1cm (⅜in) seam allowance and sew onto the marked dot – this will result in a marginally bigger box shape that should fit neatly over the base. Trim the seam allowances back to about 0.25cm (⅛in).

2 If when you slot the lid and base together, you feel it is too tight a fit, you can adjust by taking a little more seam allowance with a new line of stitching on the base, there's no need to unpick the old line.

Making and Attaching the Handle:

1 Edgestitch along both foldlines on the handle (**Fig.13**).

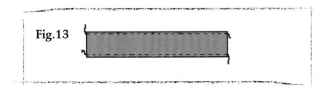

Fig.13

2 Thread a D ring (or a D ring with a base attachment as shown in **Fig.14**) onto each end and fold back about 1cm (⅜in) to the back. Sew across all thicknesses to hold the D ring in place. This can be done with a zipper foot to keep the sewing away from the bulk of the metal if you like, or hand sew through all thicknesses (**Fig. 14**).

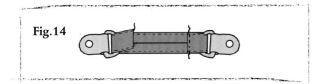

Fig.14

3 Depending on what type of D ring you have worked with, measure in 3cm or 4cm (1¼in or 1½in) from each edge of the lid that is opposite to the extension edge. Centre the handle into the width of the panel and hand sew (with double thread) through all thicknesses to secure the D ring or D ring base to the lid. This positioning will push the handle up to a nice curve for carrying (**Fig. 15**).

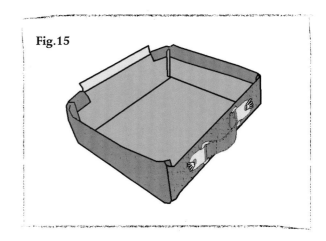

Fig.15

Sewing the Lid to the Base:

1 Position the extension edge to one of the long edges of the base. Make sure the boxes are centred to one another and make sure that the lowest part of the extension – i.e. the part at the level of the lining and interfacing – is sitting at the level of the edgestitching on the base. Pin in place and then, using double thread, hand sew the extension onto the base securely (**Fig.16**).

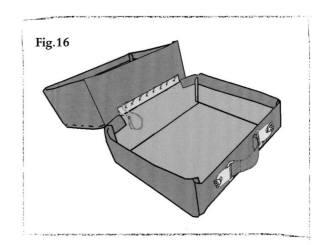

Fig.16

Luna SAVES THE Lido

Luna was lucky her job allowed her to be anywhere. Winnie and Luna had been working hard for weeks now, putting together plans to save the Lido.

All the planning permissions, the boring paper work and the go ahead from men in suits were in place. Freddie had agreed to come early to help build a catwalk. Luna couldn't wait to see him, he was always willing and had a wealth of unexpected and very useful talents. This was to be an extraordinary event.

The weekend of the show had finally arrived, and the train was due in any second; Luna and Winnie eagerly waited for it to bring the Lido heroes to them. And so it did with a toot; the sleepy seaside was soon flooded with well-dressed foxes, glamorous cats, photographers, garlands of flowers, huge balloons, benches, picnic hampers and anything else you could possibly think of. Luna was impossibly excited as she lay in bed that night making last minute lists in her head.

"Luna! Luna! Get up! You are so late! Everything has started without you! Winnie is doing her best but it's a disaster!" yelled Freddie.

Luna launched herself out of the bed and looked at the clock. 11am! She had never slept this long, and today was so important – her very best friend was relying on her to save the thing she loved!

There was still time. She thought of tiny Winnie as she dressed, how very nervous her softly spoken little friend must be! Luna threw on her jacket, and ran out the door. Even late as she was Luna couldn't help but smile at the soft rust corduroy in all it's loveliness. It was her "I mean business" jacket and business Luna Lapin did mean.

When Luna arrived everything looked marvellous, Freddie's catwalk was sturdy, the models were well dressed, a perfect contrast to the dilapidation, all frills and ball gowns, a throwback to former glory. Every possible seat was filled, the air was heavy with chatter in the Lido for the first time in a long time. It was quite something to see.

"Luna, get up here!" a wide eyed little mouse said. Luna was being pushed onto the stage, she had no time to prepare. It was fine, everything was fine. This was her moment.

And then the crowd began to laugh.

Luna looked around – what was so funny!¿! Everyone was staring at her!

"Winnie¿ Reynard¿ What is going on¿!"

"Luna, you are wearing your bloomers!"

This was a nightmare! Luna had forgotten to finish dressing!

So there she was, in front of hundreds, wearing her vintage linen bloomers and blouse and nothing else but a corduroy jacket.

"Somebody pinch me," she muttered. This wasn't a dream! This was really happening! What was a rabbit to do¿

"And now may I welcome to the stand Miss Luna Lapin, lady of the Lido, saviour of swimming pools." Brave little Winnie had taken the mike and everyone was clapping.

This was going to be okay after all. The rest of the show ran smooth as can be, everyone commented on how brave it was of Luna to show up in period dress. They praised her for the delicacy of the trim and the softness of the fabric; she was not a laughing stock but rather fashionably fierce. Luna sweetly smiled and thanked her friends.

The shoot and show made a breathtaking piece for La Clairière – the Lido was close to being saved.

Luna's Corduroy Car Coat

YOU WILL NEED

- **30cm (11¾in) x 75cm (29½in) needlecord for main fabric**
- **30cm (11¾in) x 75cm (29½in) light to quilting weight 100% cotton for lining**
- **Six 7mm (¼in) buttons**
- **Basic sewing kit (see Materials)**

Use a 0.5cm (¼in) seam allowance, unless a different amount is stated.

CUTTING OUT

1 Cut around your paper pattern pieces for the corduroy car coat carefully using scissors. I like to cut on the black line, but to the outside not the inside.

2 To cut the corduroy outer fabric, fold the fabric in half with right sides together. Pin your pattern pieces onto the fabric using **Fig.1** as a guide. Cut all pieces as stated on the pattern. Mark any triangles with a small snip to the centre – noting where there is an 'on the fold' snip. Transfer all other markings using tailor's tacks or a water-soluble pen.

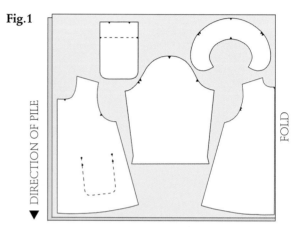

Fig.1

DIRECTION OF PILE

FOLD

3 To cut the lining fabric, fold the fabric in half with right sides together. Pin only the pattern pieces marked to be cut in lining using **Fig.2** as a guide. Mark notches and other pattern markings as for the main (outer) fabric.

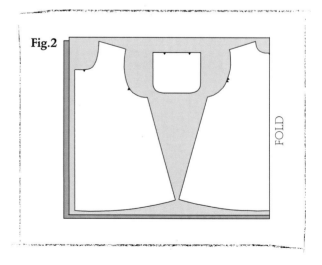

Fig.2

FOLD

MAKING UP

Making and Attaching the Pockets:

1 With right sides together, match one outer pocket with one pocket lining along the short notched straight edge. Sew to the first notch, then leave a gap and resume sewing from the second notch to the pocket edge (**Fig.3**). Press seam allowance towards the lining.

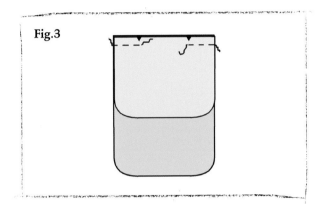

Fig.3

2 With right sides together, match up the outside edge of the outer pocket to the pocket lining – noting that the outer pocket folds back onto itself at the level of the notches to enable the outside edges to match. Sew all the way around the outside edge (**Fig.4**).

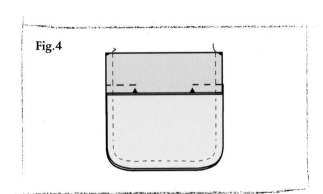

Fig.4

3 Snip off the corners of the seam allowances from the top corners and snip the seam allowances around the curves.

4 Turn the pocket through the small opening between the notches where the outer and lining are joined so that the pocket is right side out. Roll the seams out to the edges between your fingers and thumb and make sure you have pushed the corners out (use a knitting needle or similar to push out). Press flat with a warm iron. Slip stitch the opening together (see Hand Sewing Stitches: Slip Stitch) (**Fig.5**).

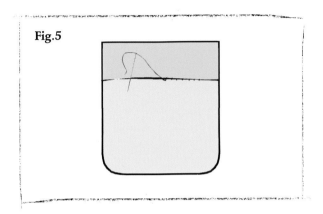

Fig.5

5 Position the pockets onto the coat front using the markings transferred from your pattern. Edgestitch (see Machine Sewing Techniques: Edgestitch) the pockets down, all the way around the outside edge of the pocket, BUT start and finish 1cm (⅜in) down from the top of the pockets (this is the lower dot position on the pattern) (**Fig.6**).

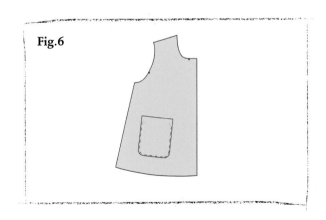

Fig.6

6 Fold down and press the 1cm (⅜in) top edge of the pocket back on itself, position a button in the centre and sew through all layers of the pocket. If your pocket flap corners are curling up, a little a spot of invisible stitching onto the pocket could happen here too (**Fig.7**).

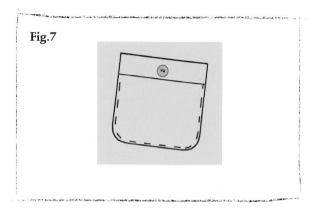

Fig.7

Sewing the Shoulder Seams in the Outer and Lining:

1 With right sides together, match the shoulder of one front to one back shoulder and sew together. Repeat with the other front and the remaining back shoulder. Press seams open (**Fig.8**). Repeat with the lining front and back (**Fig.9**).

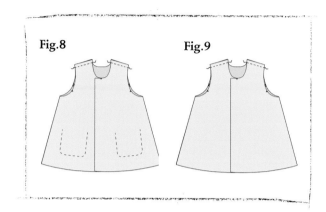

Fig.8   Fig.9

Making and Attaching the Sleeves:

1 Finish the raw edge of the sleeve hem using an overlocker or zigzag stitch on your machine. Hem the sleeves by turning 1cm (⅜in) to the wrong side. Press and sew through all layers (**Fig.10**).

Fig.10

2 Gather the top of the sleeve head between the notches (see Machine Sewing Techniques: Gathering). Don't secure either end of your gathering at this stage (**Fig.11** and **Fig.12**).

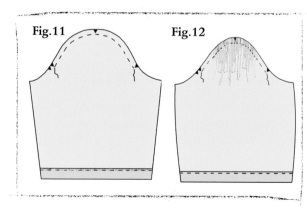

Fig.11   Fig.12

3 With right sides together, match one sleeve to one armhole of the outer coat, using the notches to position. Note the double notch denotes the back of the sleeve or the back armhole. Adjust the gathers so they are focused at the sleeve head. Pin in place and sew together (**Fig.13**).

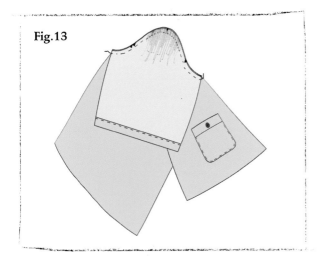

Fig.13

4 Repeat with other sleeve and armhole. Press seam allowance towards body.

Sewing the Side Seams and Underarms:
1 With right sides together, match up the armhole seams, underarms and side seams of the outer coat and pin in place. Sew together (**Fig.14**).

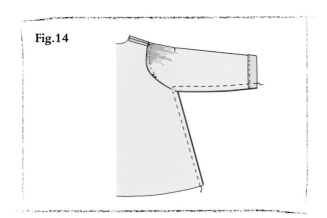

Fig.14

2 Press seams open as far as you can. Turn the coat inside out.

3 Repeat with side seams on lining, BUT on one side seam leave a gap of about 6cm (2⅜in) for turning through (**Fig.15**).

Fig.15

4 Press seams open and set aside.

Making the Collar:
1 With right sides together, pin the two collar pieces together matching the notches and sew along the long curved edge (**Fig.16**).

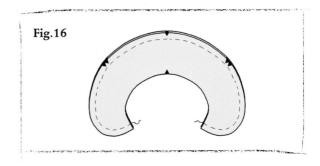

Fig.16

2 Trim the curves to reduce the bulk when you turn through.

3 Turn through to right side and press flat, ensuring the seams are right on the edge. Staystitch along the inner collar using a long stitch 0.5cm (¼in) in from the edge. Snip into the seam allowance (making sure you stop just before the staystitching) to help with the next stage (**Fig.17**).

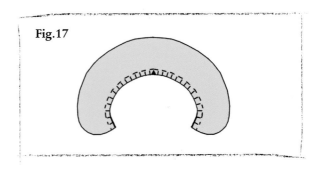

Fig.17

Sewing the Collar and Lining to the Coat:

1 With the right side of the outer coat facing you, place the collar onto the neck of the coat and position it so that the ends of the collar line up with the notches on the coat front and match the rest of the collar up with the neckline, using centre back notch as guideline. Pin and tack (baste) in place (**Fig.18**).

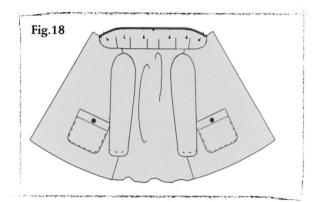

Fig.18

2 Take the lining and place it onto the outer coat with the right sides touching, matching the notches around the neck edge, front edges and hem, etc. Pin in place all the way around the coat – making sure the sleeves are safely tucked inside. Starting at one lower front edge, sew all the way around the pinned edge (**Fig.19**).

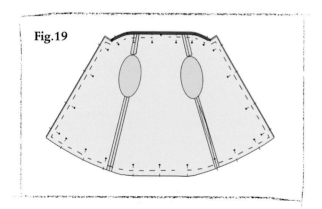

Fig.19

3 Trim any corners to reduce the bulk when you turn through and trim the neck seam allowance back to be 0.25cm (⅛in) deep. Turn the coat right sides out by gradually feeding the fabric through one lining opening. Roll the seams to be at the outside and press flat with a warm iron.

FINISHING OFF

1 After pressing all edges, edgestitch from the side seam around the front of the coat, going along the neckline to hold the seam down, and down the other front, then along the hemline, finishing where you started (see Machine Sewing Techniques: Edgestitch) (**Fig.20**).

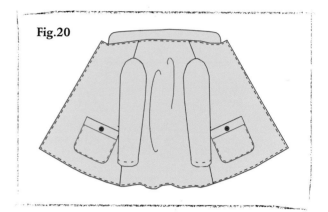

Fig.20

2 Oversew the lining armholes to the seam allowance of the sleeve armhole.

3 Slip stitch the lining side seam together.

4 Read through Making Buttonholes in Machine Sewing Techniques before you start the buttonholes.

5 Mark button and buttonhole positions along the front edges of the coat using the markings on the coat front pattern piece as a guide.

6 Make buttonholes on the right-hand side as worn.

7 Sew buttons on left-hand side as worn through both front and lining.

Luna's Bloomers

CUTTING OUT

1 Cut around your paper pattern pieces for the bloomers carefully using scissors. I like to cut on the black line, but to the outside not the inside.

2 Fold the fabric in half with right sides together. Pin your pattern pieces onto the fabric using **Fig.1** as a guide. Cut all pieces as stated on the pattern. Mark any triangles with a small snip to the centre – noting where there is an 'on the fold' snip. Mark pintuck positions using tailor's tacks or a water-soluble pen.

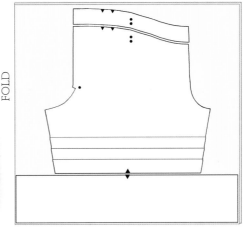

FOLD

Fig.1

YOU WILL NEED

- **60cm (24in) x 30cm (12in) linen or linen blend fabric**
- **1m (39in) of 1.5cm (⅝in) deep lace (optional)**
- **22cm (8½in) of 0.5cm (¼in) wide elastic**
- **1m (36in) of 1cm (⅜in) wide velvet ribbon**
- **Basic sewing kit (see Materials)**

Use a 0.5cm (¼in) seam allowance, unless a different amount is stated.

MAKING UP

Sewing the Pintucks:
1 With wrong sides together and working one leg at a time, press along each marked foldline for the pintucks and sew about 0.25cm (⅛in) in from the fold. Press each set of pintucks so that they face away from each other and lay towards each side seam (**Fig.2**).

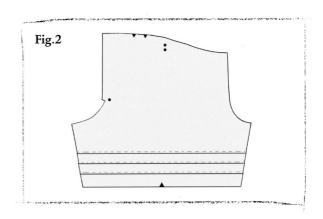

Fig.2

Making and Attaching the Lower Leg Frills:

1 Make the hems on the lower leg frills by turning 0.5cm (¼in) to the wrong side and then a further 1cm (⅜in) to enclose the raw edges. Press and stitch in place (**Fig.3**).

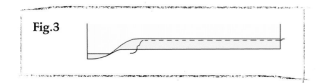

Fig.3

2 Attach the optional lace at this point. Pin it in place so that it sits approx. 0.25cm (⅛in) onto the wrong side of the hem. Tack (baste) in place first, then using an edgestitch sew in place with a machine (see Machine Sewing Techniques: Edgestitch). Alternatively you can sew it in place with an invisible hand stitch.

3 Gather along the top un-hemmed edge of each of the leg frills, don't secure your gathering until the next step (see Machine Sewing Techniques: Gathering) (**Fig.4**).

Fig.4

4 With right sides together, match the gathered top of each leg frill to the lower edge of each of the legs of the bloomers. Adjust your gathers to be evenly spread and match notches. Sew in place (**Fig.5**).

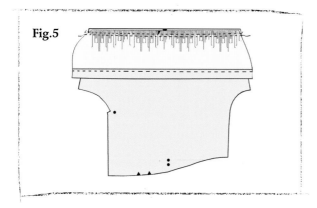

Fig.5

5 Remove any visible gathering threads and press the seam allowance upwards away from the frill.

Sewing the Inside Leg Seams:

1 Work one leg at a time. With right sides together, fold the leg along the length and pin the inside leg seams together making sure the seamline for the lower frill matches up on each side and sew. Repeat with the other leg (**Fig.6**). Press the seams open as well as you can – it won't be easy unless you have a mini iron!

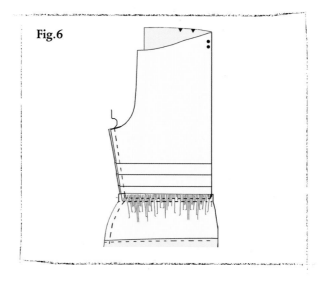

Fig.6

Sewing the Crotch Seam:

1 Turn one leg right side out and slide it (hem edge first) inside the other leg to sew the crotch. Match the inside leg seams and the extension seam allowance at the back. Pin and sew the crotch. Only sew up to the marked spot along the back to leave an opening for the tail (**Fig.7**).

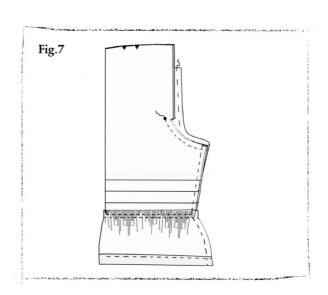

Fig.7

Making and Attaching the Waist Facing:

1 With right sides together, sew together the short ends at the front of the waist facing pieces and press open (**Fig.8**). (To identify which ends are the front, they are the ones furthest away from the double notches along the top of the waist facings.)

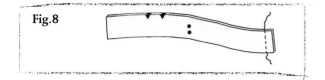

Fig.8

2 Zigzag or overlock around the lower un-notched edge of the facing to finish.

3 With the bloomers right side out, place the waist facing over the waist of the bloomers with the right sides together; match up the edges of the waist to the facing using the notches (there are double notches along the back waist); match the centre front seams and sew the facing to the bloomers. Press the seam allowance up, towards the facing (**Fig.9**).

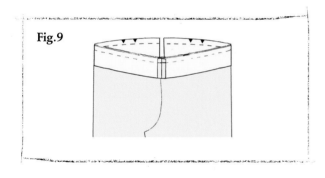

Fig.9

4 At the centre back, press 1cm (⅜in) seam allowances towards the wrong side and sew in place approx. 0.5cm (¼in) from the folded edge (**Fig.10**).

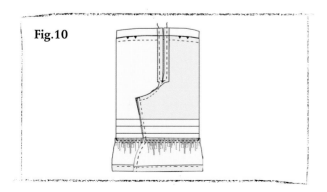

Fig.10

Making the Casing:

1 Turn the waist facing to the inside of the bloomers, press and pin in place. Edgestitch around the top edge, then topstitch 1cm (⅜in) down from the edgestitching (see Machine Sewing Techniques: Edgestitch and Machine Sewing Techniques: Topstitch) (**Fig.11**).

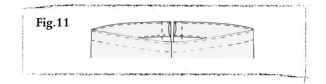

Fig.11

2 Cut a piece of elastic 8cm (3¼in) long. Cut the velvet ribbon in half. Overlap one end of each piece of ribbon over each end of the elastic by 1cm (⅜in) and join together with a zigzag stitch or hand stitch (**Fig.12**).

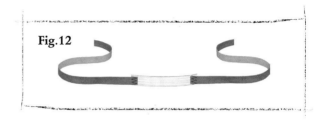

Fig.12

3 Pop a safety pin through one end of one piece of ribbon and close the pin.

4 Thread the ribbon and the elastic through the waist casing using your safety pin, ensuring that the unthreaded end of the elastic/ribbon is still accessible.

5 Pull through until the elastic is centred to the centre front seam and position your elastic/ribbon overlap so that it is level with the side marker dots – and stitch through from the edgestitching to the casing lower stitching to keep the elastic at the front of the bloomers. Ensure the elastic is lying flat before you stitch the other side in the same way with the other elastic/ribbon join (**Fig.13**).

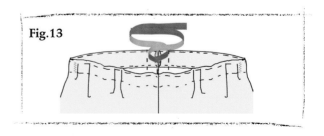

Fig.13

6 To wear, tie the velvet ribbons together around the waist.

Luna
AND THE *big dress* PROJECT

"What a day!" said Luna, collapsing into her big, comfortable bed. La Clairière had been rife with gossip, rumour was that Lupine (only the most fashionable design house in town) was on the hunt for a new designer, and not only was it a hunt, they had bought a 4-page spread in the magazine advertising the competition that was going to help them find their new star!

Luna knew she just had to enter – if anyone had a shot it was Luna Lapin, the quiet and kind rabbit who achieved remarkable things in wonderful clothing. Luna had just one chance to create the perfect dress. She picked up her pencil and began to draw, pieces of paper soon discarded on the floor.

"No, no, no," she thought. "This isn't right, tomorrow is another day," and she drifted off to sleep.

Luna woke up inspired, she would design a dress for Clementine. Clementine was the most stylish cat Luna had ever met. Clementine had fiery orange fur tipped with white, and liked to joke that she dressed for every one of her nine lives. There was once a rumour that Clementine was the great-great-great granddaughter of Dixie Lincoln, the cat who was smarter than an entire cabinet. It would be quite unlikely after meeting Clementine that you would find this rumour to be false. She was as cunning a cat as she was kind.

"Hello you," said the coolest of cats, "what can I do to help?"

Luna took a seat and explained how desperately she wanted to win this competition, how desperately she wanted to be a fashion designer, and how very desperately she wanted to design a dress for Clem, a dress to end all dresses.

"It should be BIG!"

"It should feel fantastic, and expensive, there should be velvet!"

Luna sat and listened to all the requests, her pencil scribbling away the whole time. Finally, she was done. Luna presented the design to Clementine.

"That is it, Luna! You marvellous girl! That is the most dreamy of dresses."

And it truly was. It was sleeveless and heavily frosted with layers upon layers of tulle. Luna set out to her favourite haberdashery, on a little street that hung its dress samples on the gate. It had fabric folded into stars swinging from the ceiling. It was an enchanting place, brimming with all kinds of delights, with buttons more delectable than sweets.

Luna pulled out reams of fabric, every texture, print and colour imaginable. For the skirt, Luna picked peaches and reds so it would give the impression the wearer was a walking peony. For the top, a softly coloured floral that ripples when touched. She completed the whole thing with the most luxurious deep velvet ribbon imaginable. Luna couldn't wait to start stitching this gown.

It took Luna three whole days to have the dress just right – even our crafty little rabbit struggles sometimes. But when it was done it really was something to behold.

Luna was so nervous for the judging; her photos had made it through the first round but it didn't stop her paws from shaking. What if she wasn't good enough? What if her dress wasn't what they were looking for? What if, what if, what if?

The light wouldn't stop flashing and it was so very loud. Luna felt dizzy, faint even. And then there was quiet, dark, a thud and nothing.

Luna awoke to a roar of clapping. Alfie's face was right in front of her.

"Luna. You WON!"

"I won?!?! I really won!"

Luna stood herself up and walked onstage.

It was official. Luna would be the new in-house designer for Lupine. She would miss her friends at La Clairière so very much, but she had made it – Luna Lapin was a star.

Clementine's Dreamy Dress

CUTTING OUT

1 Cut around your paper pattern pieces for the dreamy dress carefully using scissors. I like to cut on the black line, but to the outside not the inside.

2 Fold the bodice fabric in half with right sides together. Pin your pattern pieces onto the fabric using **Fig.1** as a guide. Cut all pieces as stated on the pattern. Mark any triangles with a small snip to the centre. Mark press stud positions using tailor's tacks or a water-soluble pen.

FOLD

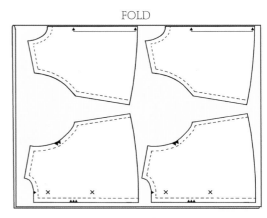

Fig.1

3 Cut tulle so you have two panels each measuring 21cm (8¼in) x 150cm (59in) for all three colours, making six panels in total.

MAKING UP

Sewing the Ribbon onto the Front Bodice:

1 Cut a 12cm (4¾in) piece off the ribbon. Lay the ribbon face up onto the right side, down the centre of the bodice front. Edgestitch down both edges (see Machine Sewing Techniques: Edgestitch) (**Fig.2**).

YOU WILL NEED

- **30cm (11¾in) x 30cm (11¾in) light to quilting weight 100% cotton for the bodice**
- **1m (39½in) of 2cm (¾in) wide velvet ribbon**
- **0.5m (19¾in) of three different colours of tulle each 150cm (59in) wide for the skirt**
- **Two press studs**
- **Basic sewing kit (see Materials)**

Use a 0.5cm (¼in) seam allowance, unless a different amount is stated.

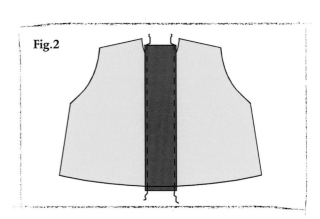

Fig.2

2 Trim the ribbon to match the shape of the neckline of the top (**Fig.3**).

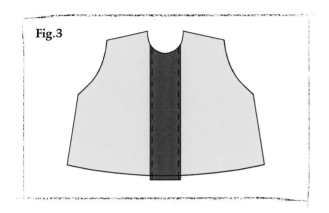

Fig.3

Sewing the Shoulder Seams:

1 With right sides together, match the shoulder seam of one back to one front shoulder seam and sew.

2 Repeat with the other back and the remaining front shoulder seam (**Fig.4**). Press seams open.

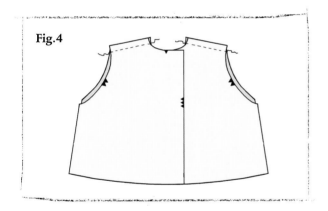

Fig.4

3 Repeat this stage with the front and back lining pieces.

Sewing the Back Edges and Neckline:

1 With right sides together, match the edges of the lining up to the outer pieces around the neckline and back edges.

2 Pin in place and starting at the lower edge of one back, sew around the edges of each centre back and around the neck finishing at the other lower back (see Machine Sewing Techniques: Coping with Curves) (**Fig.5**).

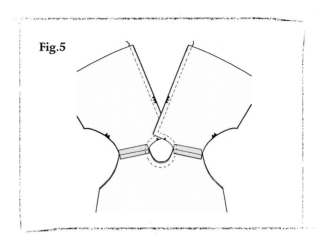

Fig.5

3 Trim excess seam allowances at the corners and snip into the seam allowance at the neck curve to allow the seam allowance to sit flat once turned (but don't turn through yet!).

Sewing the Armholes:

1 Pin lining to main fabric around each armhole, matching the shoulder seams and edges, and sew in place (**Fig.6**).

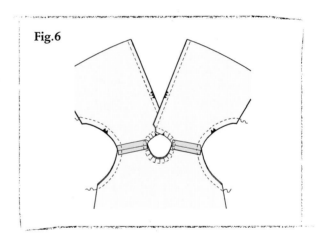

Fig.6

2 Snip into the seam allowances on the armholes to allow the seam allowances to sit flat once turned.

Turning the Bodice Right Side Out:

1 Push each back through the opening of the shoulder seam to the front and turn through (**Fig.7**).

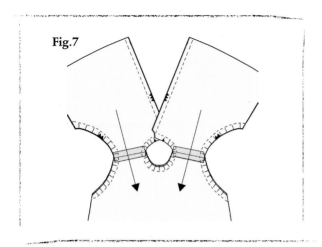

Fig.7

2 Use a knitting needle or chopstick to push out the corners. Roll the edges between your fingers and thumb to get the seams on the edge and press the top back, neck edge and armholes flat (**Fig.8**).

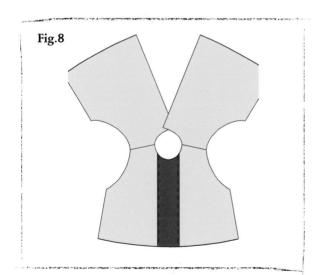

Fig.8

Sewing the Side Seams:

1 Working one side at a time and with right sides together, match and pin one front side seam to one back side seam (of the outer only), open out the lining and continue across the armhole seam onto the front and back linings. Make sure that the armhole seams match. Sew this side seam and repeat with the other side seam (**Fig.9**).

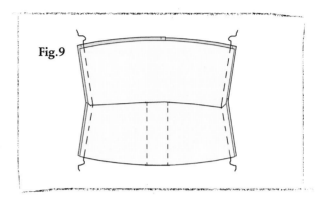

Fig.9

Making the Skirt:

1 Layer up the tulle pieces so that the order of colours is lightest at the bottom, next the mid tone and then the darkest, and repeat again in the same order. Put some large pins in to hold all the layers together along the top long edge.

2 Gather the top edge of the skirt (see Machine Sewing Techniques: Gathering) and draw up the gathers until the skirt measures 31cm (12¼in).

Sewing the Skirt to the Bodice:

1 With right sides together, match the gathered top of the skirt to the lower edge of the outer bodice. Adjust your gathers to be even and keep the bodice lining out of the way. Sew together (**Fig.10**).

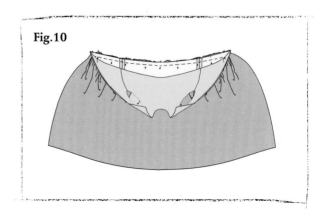

Fig.10

2 Fold up the 1cm (⅜in) seam allowance along the lower edge of the lining to the wrong side and match and pin to the seamline on the skirt.

3 Slip stitch in place by hand to enclose all raw edges (see Hand Sewing Stitches: Slip Stitch) (**Fig.11** and **Fig.12**).

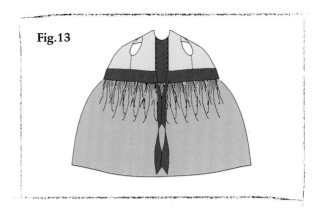

Fig.13

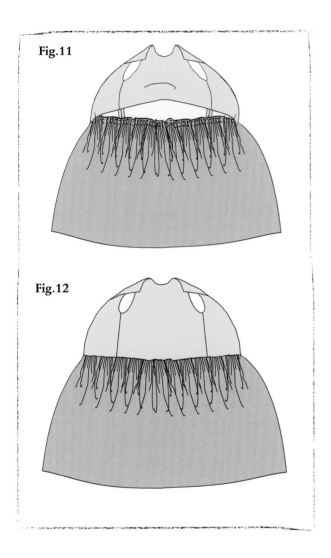

Fig.11

Fig.12

Sewing the Back Seam:

1 Match up all the tulle layers along each back edge, then with right sides together sew up the back of the skirt using a 1cm (⅜in) seam allowance. Stop 1cm (⅜in) below the waist seam (**Fig.14**).

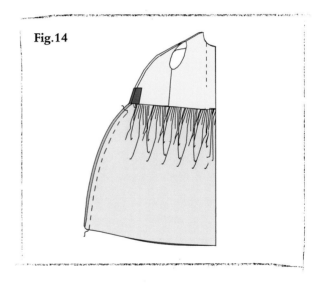

Fig.14

2 Turn the dress to be right sides out and sew press studs onto the back opening of the bodice using the previously marked positions. The left-hand side as worn will overlap the right-hand side. Tie the ribbons in a knot or bow to finish.

Sewing the Ribbon Tie:

1 Cut the remaining ribbon in half and pin in place on the waist, starting at the edges of the central ribbon trim. Fold 1cm (⅜in) in around the bodice back opening so the raw edges are hidden and position the lower edge of the ribbon so it sits just below the waist seam. Slip stitch each lower edge in place working from the back around to the front and stopping when you reach the level of the vertical ribbon on the bodice. Repeat with the top edge (**Fig.13**).

Frame Top Bag

YOU WILL NEED

- Scrap of felt about 10cm (4in) wide by 20cm (8in) long
- Metal sew on purse frame – mouth to measure 5cm (2in) across
- Six-stranded embroidery cotton (floss) or perle cotton
- Two diamante beads 0.5cm (¼in) diameter
- Basic sewing kit (see Materials)

Use a 0.5cm (¼in) seam allowance, unless a different amount is stated.

CUTTING OUT

1 Cut around your paper pattern pieces for the frame top bag carefully using scissors. I like to cut on the black line, but to the outside not the inside.

2 Cut your bag piece twice from the felt. Mark any triangles with a small snip to the centre. Also cut one large flower, two medium flowers and two small flowers from the felt.

MAKING UP

Sewing the Outer:

1 With right sides together, match the edges of the two felt bag pieces, pin in place and sew around the bottom of the bag. You can do this on a sewing machine or by using a backstitch (see Hand Sewing Stitches: Backstitch) (**Fig.1**).

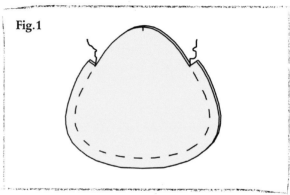

Fig.1

2 Turn the bag right sides out so the seam allowance is to the inside (**Fig.2**).

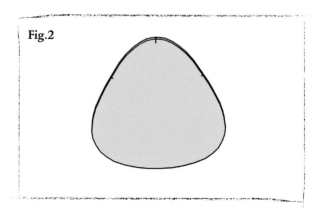

Fig.2

Sewing the Bag to the Frame:

1 Thread your needle with the six strands of an embroidery thread or perle cotton and knot the long end twice to form a substantial knot.

2 On the right-hand side of one felt piece, secure your thread to the top of the seam allowance on the inside of the bag. Push the needle through to the right side 0.5cm (¼in) up from join and 0.5cm (¼in) in from the cut edge.

3 Open the frame as wide as it can go. Pass the threaded needle through the second hole of the purse frame, and pull the felt tight into the U shape on the underside of the frame (**Fig.3**).

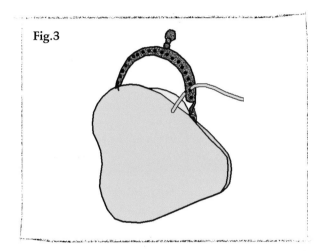

Fig.3

4 Now sew down through the first hole to the wrong side, ensuring you also travel through the felt and come up through the third hole to the right side again.

5 Sew through to the back through the second hole and continue sewing this backstitch around the whole of the frame edge. You will find getting started more difficult than the rest of the sewing but persevere (**Fig.4**).

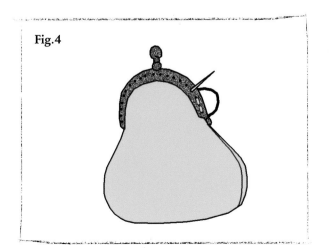

Fig.4

6 Check that the small notch at the top of the felt bag shape lines up with the centre of the frame. Using a small piece of adhesive tape around the frame and fabric will help to hold them in this position.

7 Watch out for the thread getting caught around the purse bobbles. Fasten off with a few small stitches in the same place when you have completed one side. Repeat with the second side, taping and then sewing. Trim all ends of the cotton (**Fig.5**).

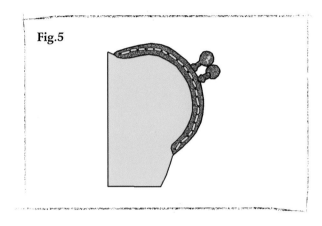

Fig.5

FINISHING OFF

1 Push the shape of the bag out with your fingers and find a few positions for your flowers; attach them by layering two or three of different sizes on top of each other and sewing through the centres leaving the petals free. Then sew some diamante beads in the centre to cover your original stitching (**Fig.6**).

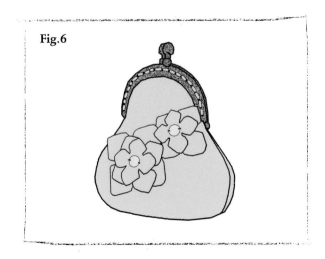

Fig.6

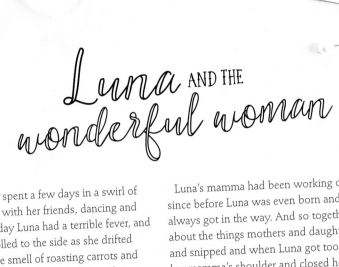

Luna AND THE wonderful woman

Following her win, Luna spent a few days in a swirl of excitement, celebrating with her friends, dancing and living a fine life. But today Luna had a terrible fever, and her sleepy little head lolled to the side as she drifted in between wake and sleep. The smell of roasting carrots and honey woke her, floating into her nostrils, and making them flutter in the special way that rabbits' noses do. This smell could only mean one thing. "Hello, little one," said Mamma Lapin, bringing her a bowl of bright orange soup. "How are you feeling?"

Luna smiled the soft sweet smile of childhood, remembering all the times she had been ever so small and ever so sick. She remembered the way her mamma had stroked her head and told her she would be well enough to play outside with her brother Alfie in no time at all. Luna was so glad she was here.

Mamma Lapin was a wonder with a sewing machine, the things she created seemed like bird song in fabric form. She made the best mushrooms on toast any rabbit had ever known. Her upside-down pear cake had won awards for its perfect golden crust. Luna was incredibly proud of her Mamma Lapin. She was always busy but always magical.

"I thought I should come take care of you and maybe we could finish this." Mama pulled out a box full of hexagonal pieces so delicate that they looked like thousands of petals. It was a quilt, but not just any quilt! It was <u>the</u> quilt.

Luna's mamma had been working on the same patchwork since before Luna was even born and somehow something had always got in the way. And so together they sat and, talking about the things mothers and daughters talk about, they stitched and snipped and when Luna got too tired she rested her head on her mamma's shoulder and closed her eyes.

These lazy days filled with getting better and love were some of the best Luna could imagine; it was almost worth such a terrible cold to see the fairy tales of her childhood joining up next to the scraps of her favourite dresses, each one pieced together with the warmth that kinship brings.

After Luna's mamma went home, Luna climbed back into bed. Tomorrow she would be back at work; she looked forward to the hustle of the office, to Reynard's joking around, to Clem's beautiful studio and all of the wonderful stories she told. But tonight she was just happy to be in her big soft bed, in her cosiest nightie and to be sleeping for the very first time under her quilt. Luna would treasure this quilt. Even though she was so very far from the warren she grew up in, the memory of great love was stitched in to every piece.

Luna's Nightie

YOU WILL NEED

- **71cm (28in) x 50cm (19¾in) light to quilting weight 100% cotton**
- **One 7mm (¼in) doll button**
- **Basic sewing kit (see Materials)**

Use a 0.5cm (¼in) seam allowance, unless a different amount is stated.

CUTTING OUT

1 Cut around your paper pattern pieces for the nightie carefully using scissors. I like to cut on the black line, but to the outside not the inside.

2 Fold the fabric in half so long edges are together and so that right sides are together. Pin your pattern pieces onto the fabric using **Fig.1** as a guide. Cut all pieces as stated on the pattern. Mark any triangles with a small snip to the centre.

Fig.1

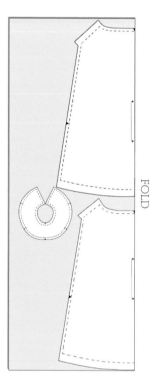

FOLD

MAKING UP

Making the Yoke:

1 With right sides together, match and pin around the back edges and neck edge on the yoke pieces. Sew together (**Fig.2**).

Fig.2

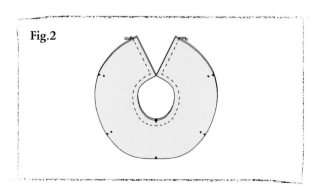

2 Trim excess seam allowance away at corners and snip into the curve of the neck edge to allow the neck to sit flat when turned through. Match and pin the outer edge between the marked dots only. Sew together being careful to start and stop where the marked dots are on the pieces (**Fig.3**).

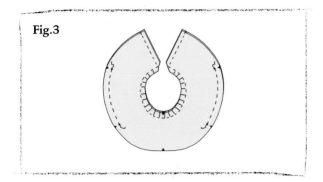

Fig.3

3 Snip to the dots, i.e. down to the level of the sewing line. Turn the yoke through to the right side, poking corners out gently with a knitting needle and rolling the seams to the edge between your fingers and thumbs. Make sure the seam allowance is visible up to the sewing point on the armhole areas. Press flat (**Fig.4**).

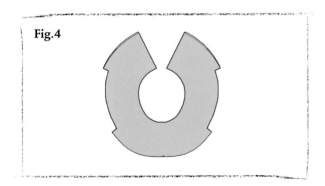

Fig.4

4 Sew the doll button onto the right-hand side (as worn) of the back opening on the yoke, positioning 0.5cm (¼in) in and down from the corner.

5 Create a hand sewn button loop on the left-hand edge. To do this work with a double thread on your needle and knot the end. Come in through the layers so the knot is enclosed and so the thread comes out just below the corner of the back yoke (point A). Sew back into the yoke edge 0.75cm (⁵⁄₁₆in) down (point B) and then bring your needle back out at point A. Don't pull your thread tight – you are looking to make a loop that is big enough to pass over the button – so probably leave 1cm (⅜in) of thread sitting in the loop and now bring the needle down to B (**Fig.5**).

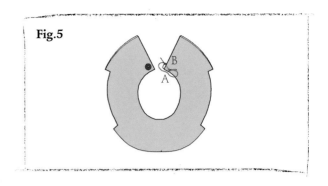

Fig.5

6 Strengthen the loop by working a blanket stitch (see Hand Sewing Techniques: Blanket Stitch) around the four threads. Pass the needle through the loop and bring the thread around the back of the needle. Slowly draw the thread tight and the knot will sit around the loop. Repeat along the length of the loop – the blanket stitches should sit alongside one another. If you find the needle thread is twisting, allow it to dangle to untangle. When you arrive at the base of the loop, secure with a couple of small stitches (**Fig.6**). Keep yoke unfastened for now. Check the back yoke edges are the same length – trim if necessary.

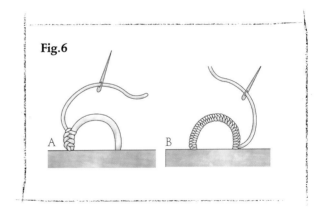

Fig.6

Sewing the Armholes and Neck:
1 On the front panel, turn the armhole edges to the wrong side by 0.5cm (¼in) and then by a further 0.5cm (¼in). Press and edgestitch in place. Repeat with back armholes (**Fig.7**).

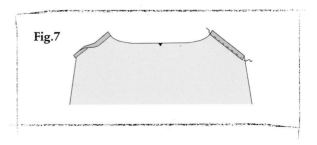

Fig.7

2 Gather the front and back top edges (see Machine Sewing Techniques: Gathering) (**Fig.8**).

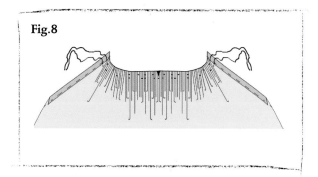

Fig.8

Sewing the Yoke to the Nightie:

1 With right sides together, match the gathered top of the front to the lower edge of the front yoke. It is important that the ends match up neatly. Adjust your gathers to be evenly spread and match up the centre front notches. Sew through all layers. Remove any visible gathering threads and press the seam allowances up towards the yoke (**Fig.9**).

2 Butt the finished back edges of the back yoke to one another and hand sew together 0.5cm (¼in) up from the raw edges.

3 With right sides together, match the gathered top of the back to the lower edge of the back yoke. Adjust your gathers to be evenly spread so that the centre notch matches up to where the back yokes join. Sew through all layers (**Fig.10**).

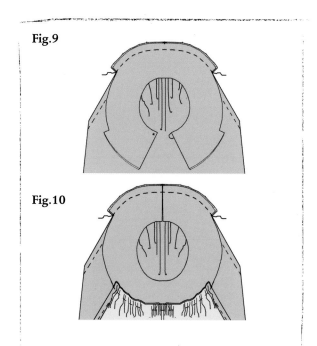

Fig.9

Fig.10

4 Remove any visible gathering threads and press the seam allowances up towards the yoke.

Sewing the Side Seams:

1 With right sides together, match and pin the side seams. Sew together and finish the raw edges with a zigzag stitch or overlocker. Press seam allowances towards the back of the nightie (**Fig.11**).

Fig.11

Sewing the Hem:

1 To make the hem, turn up 0.5cm (¼in) to the wrong side and press, then turn up a further 1cm (⅜in) and edgestitch (see Machine Sewing Techniques: Edgestitch) in place (**Fig.12**).

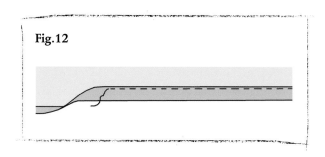

Fig.12

Mattress

Firstly measure the bed surface width and length. The one we have used is 30cm (11¾in) x 47cm (18½in).

CUTTING OUT

1 Cut two pieces of fabric 32cm (12½in) x 49cm (19¼in) to make a top and a base for your mattress. NOTE: If the surface of your bed is different from ours, you will need to change the size of these pieces: use the length (plus two lots of seam allowance) and width (plus two lots of seam allowance) of your bed surface to work out the dimensions to cut your mattress top and base.

2 Cut two pieces of fabric 79cm (31⅛in) x 7cm (2¾in) to make side panels for your mattress. NOTE: If the surface of your bed and the depth of your foam are different from ours, you will need to change the size of these pieces: use the length of your bed surface plus the width of your bed surface (plus two lots of seam allowance) to work out the length of your side panels. Then use the depth of your foam (plus two lots of seam allowance) to work out the width of your side panels.

3 Your shapes will look roughly like **Fig.1** when marked out on 115cm (45in) wide fabric laid flat.

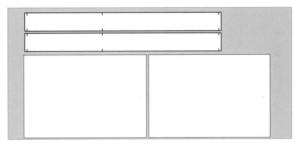

Fig.1

4 Prepare the mattress top and base by marking the seamlines 1cm (⅜in) in from the corners and a dot at the corners where the seamlines intersect.

5 Fuse some of the fabric left over after cutting out your mattress with iron-on interfacing and cut out 16 circles each 2cm (¾in) in diameter (see The Patterns: Mattress, Tufting Circle).

YOU WILL NEED

- **50cm (19¾in) of 115cm (45in) wide striped 100% quilting weight cotton**
- **5cm (2in) deep foam measuring 30cm (11¾in) x 47cm (18½in) – depending on your bed size**
- **5cm (2in) x 12.5cm (5in) medium weight iron-on interfacing**
- **Basic sewing kit (see Materials)**

Use a 0.5cm (¼in) seam allowance, unless a different amount is stated.

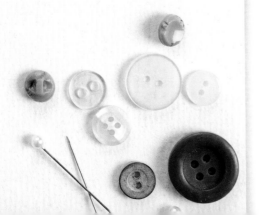

MAKING UP

Making the Side Panels:

1 With right sides together, join the side panels at one of the short ends. Start and finish the seam 1cm (⅜in) in from the long edges (**Fig.2**). Press open (**Fig.3**).

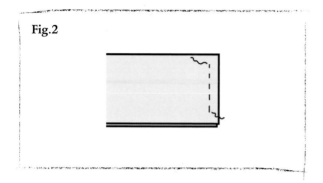

Fig.2

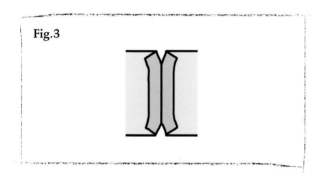

Fig.3

2 Put some notches into the long edges of the side panel to help with the insertion. Starting from the left and with wrong side facing upwards snip both upper and lower edges at 1cm (⅜in) in from the short edge, then make another set of notches 30cm (11¾in) (or your bed width) from the first notches, then 47cm (18½in) (or your bed length) from that should be your seam SO NO NEED TO SNIP, then 30cm (11¾in) (or your bed width) along from the seam and then at 47cm (18½in) (or your bed length) along from the last set of notches. This should leave you 1cm (⅜in) seam allowance at the end. At each point snip into the fabric by 0.75cm (⁵⁄₁₆in), unless it's a seam (**Fig.4**).

Sewing the Side Panel to the Mattress Top:

1 Lay the mattress top with the right side facing upwards in front of you with a shorter edge at the top. Lay the side panel, right side down so the short end of the side panel lines up with the top left of the mattress top. Starting 1cm (⅜in) in from the short end of the side panel, at the level of the snip, sew along the top until you are at the dot at the next corner of the mattress top. This should line up with the snip in the side panel (**Fig.5**).

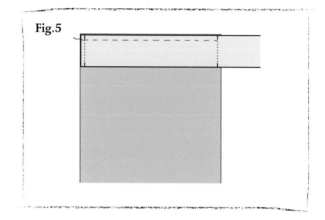

Fig.5

2 Leaving the needle in the machine, lift your machine foot and move the long strip to a 90-degree angle, pivot and line up the next edge. The snip next to your pivot will open up. Stitch along this edge – hopefully you will find that your seam lines up with the next corner dot – and pivot at the notch (**Fig.6**).

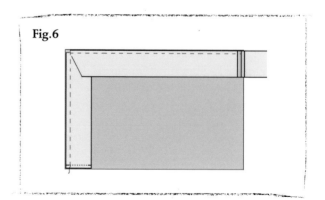

Fig.6

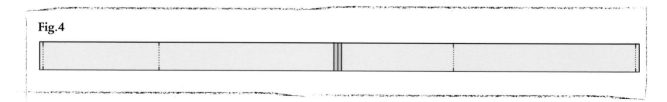

Fig.4

3 Continue along the remaining two edges, making sure when you reach the last edge that the start of the side panel is out of the way. Finish sewing 1cm (⅜in) before the end of the side panel (**Fig.7**).

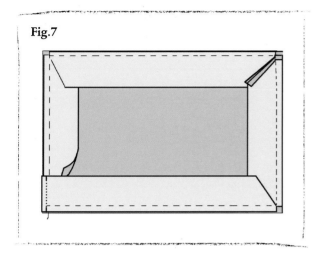

Fig.7

Sewing the Ends of the Side Panel:
1 Take the two short ends of the side panel and pin, then sew together, starting and finishing 1cm (⅜in) in from the edges (**Fig.8**).

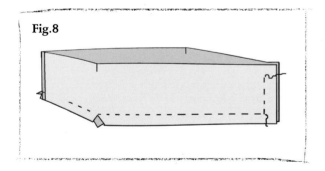

Fig.8

Sewing on the Mattress Base:
1 Take the remaining mattress panel and with right sides together attach the base in the same way as the top. Match up the shape to the free side panel edge and sew on in the same way using the corner spots as a guide and the notches to pivot. This time, however, leave the last edge open to turn and fill the mattress (**Fig.9** and **Fig.10**).

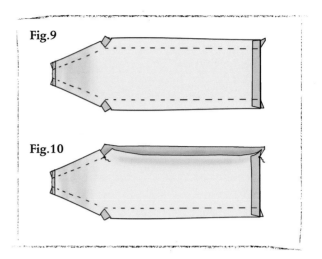

Fig.9

Fig.10

2 Turn the mattress to be right sides out. Bend your foam in half along the length and push it into the cover (this is a struggle but focus on getting the two far corners in first and everything then becomes okay). Slip stitch the two edges together to seal the mattress (see Hand Sewing Techniques: Slip Stitch) (**Fig.11**).

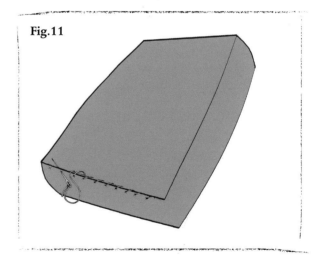

Fig.11

Making the Mattress Tufts:
1 To make Luna's mattress look a little more authentic we will sew through all layers to create an effect of 'hand tufting'. With the mattress top facing upwards, measure 8cm (3⅛in) in from each of the corners. Now measure the distance between these points and mark half way between. Use a ruler to find the diagonal points between your marks and mark them as well. This gives eight points for sewing. Using a strong thread, at least a double normal thread, fasten your thread onto the mattress top at one of the marked points (**Fig.12**).

Fig.12

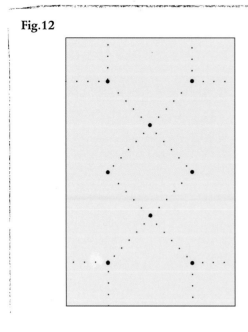

2 Take a small circle and pass the needle through and bring the small circle down so it is sitting right sides upwards on the mattress. Bring the needle down through the circle, straight through the mattress and pick up another circle on the base. Continue to sew through the layers pulling the thread tight to draw in the mattress. Fasten off on the fabric on the base of the mattress. Repeat this step with the other marked points and the remaining circles (**Fig.13**).

Fig.13

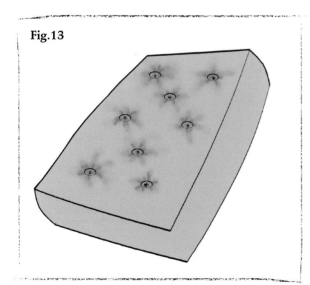

Pillows and Sheet

YOU WILL NEED
(To make two pillows and one sheet)

- **60cm (23½in) of 115cm (45in) wide light to quilting weight 100% cotton**
- **Four 7mm (¼in) doll buttons**
- **Small amount of toy stuffing**
- **Basic sewing kit (see Materials)**

The bed we have used for Luna is 30cm (11¾in) x 47cm (18½in), if you have a bed that is much bigger than this you may need to adjust the sheet dimensions and make four pillows for a double bed.

CUTTING OUT

1 To make two pillows, cut two rectangles 12cm (4¾in) x 42cm (16½in).

2 To make one sheet, cut one rectangle 56cm (22in) x 73cm (28¾in).

MAKING UP

Sewing the Hems on the Pillows:
1 With wrong side facing upwards, turn 1cm (⅜in) to wrong side at one short end and edgestitch in place. Turn the other short end in by 1cm (⅜in) and then 1cm (⅜in) to the wrong side and edgestitch in place (see Machine Sewing Techniques: Edgestitch) (**Fig.1**).

Fig.1

Sewing the Long Edges of the Pillows:
1 Turn the strip over to be right side upwards and bring the double folded end in by 14cm (5½in). If your pillow is bigger or smaller than ours, adjust this number respectively. Then bring the single folded end over so that it overlaps the other end by 3cm (1¼in) and press. End to folded end, the pillowcase should now measure 18cm (7in) (**Fig.2** and **Fig.3**).

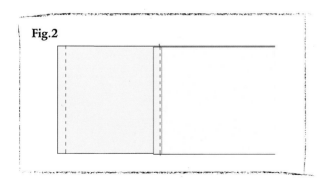
Fig.2

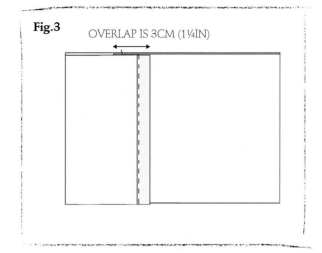
Fig.3
OVERLAP IS 3CM (1¼IN)

2 Pin along the top and bottom edges and sew using a 1cm (⅜in) seam allowance. Trim excess off corners and turn through. Push corners out to be sharp using a knitting needle or similar. Roll seams out to edges and press flat (**Fig.4**).

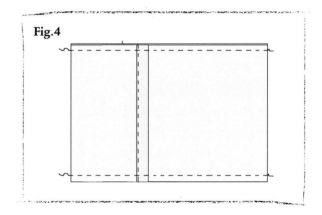
Fig.4

Making the Border on the Pillows:
1 Topstitch 2cm (¾in) in from all edges on the right side to create an Oxford pillowcase (**Fig.5**).

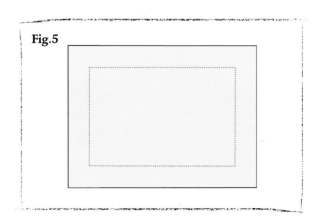
Fig.5

2 Fill with stuffing ensuring you get some into the corners. Smooth out the opening you have used to stuff the case. Sew a couple of buttons onto the overlap to fasten it down **(Fig.6)**.

Sewing the Hems on the Sheet:
1 On each long edge, turn and press 1cm (⅜in) to the wrong side **(Fig.7)** and then a further 1cm (⅜in). Edgestitch in place (see Machine Sewing Techniques: Edgestitch) **(Fig.8)**.

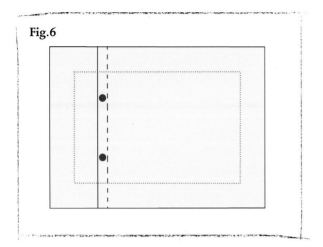

Fig.6

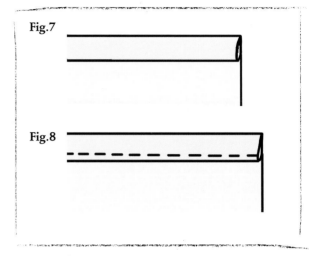

Fig.7

Fig.8

3 Repeat to make second pillowcase.

2 Repeat with the short edges. Trim thread ends and press well **(Fig.9** and **Fig.10)**.

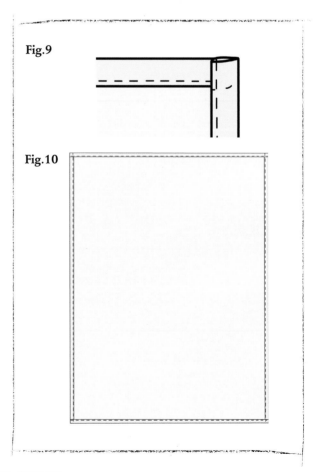

Fig.9

Fig.10

PILLOWS AND SHEET

YOU WILL NEED

- **A selection of quilting weight cottons – fat quarters in six different but tonal prints and 0.5m (19¾in) of a soft (non-optic) white quilting weight cotton for the background**
- **One fat quarter of a print or plain for the quilt backing**
- **One fat quarter of wadding**
- **You might like to use quilting cotton thread, and a pressing cloth to press the quilt top.**
- **200 2cm (¾in) hexagonal papers – there is a template for these in The Patterns section – or you may want to download online, or buy ready cut paper pieces. Die cutting systems are also available to cut both papers and fabrics**
- **Basic sewing kit (see Materials)**

CUTTING OUT

1 Cut your six fat quarters of printed fabric into 4cm (1½in) squares:

- Flower 1 needs 24 colour A and 4 colour B (makes 4 flowers)

- Flower 2 needs 18 colour C and 3 colour D (makes 3 flowers)

- Flower 3 needs 18 colour E and 3 colour F (makes 3 flowers)

2 Cut your white background fabric into 128 4cm (1½in) squares of which 16 should be cut in half to be sewn as half hexagons.

MAKING UP

Making a Hexagon:
1 Place a hexagon paper onto the wrong side of a fabric square (**Fig.1**).

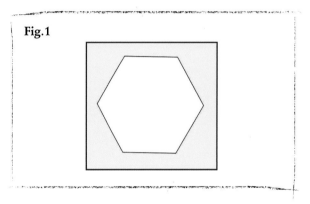

Fig.1

2 I like to fold over the top edge of the fabric first and then fold the next edge, working anticlockwise. The fold in the fabric needs to be tight against the edge of the paper without distorting the paper (**Fig.2**).

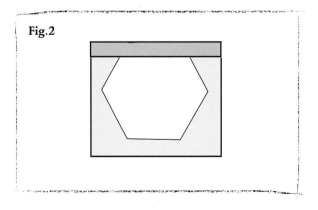

Fig.2

3 Where the edge of the second fold meets the first, secure your thread and take a stitch through all the layers to hold the fabric to the paper and the folds in place (**Fig.3**).

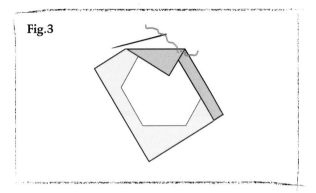

Fig.3

4 Fold the third edge of the hexagon and sew this folded corner down (**Fig.4**).

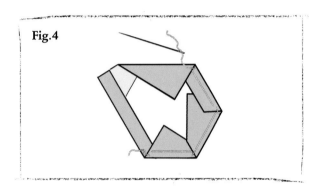

Fig.4

5 Repeat all the way around the edge until you have completed the shape (**Fig.5**).

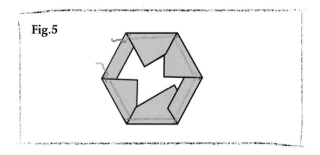

Fig.5

6 Secure your sewing, but this is only tacking (basting) and it will have to be pulled out eventually. You don't need to go through the paper to the other side of the piece but this is a process to be repeated over and over again so you will find your own preferred way.

Sewing the Hexagons Together:

1 The next step is to sew the individual hexagons together. For this design, take the centre piece of each 'flower' and line up a surrounding colour hexagon, with right sides together. Whipstitch the edges together with small tight stitches (see Hand Sewing Techniques: Overstitch/Whipstitch) (**Fig.6**).

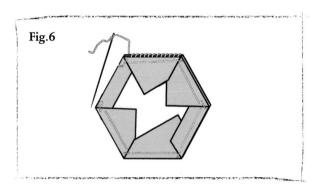

Fig.6

2 When you get to the end of this edge, add another hexagon and sew with right sides together – until you have added a hexagon to each edge of the central hexagon. To complete, sew two touching edges of the outer colour together and fasten off securely. Then sew each of the remaining edges of the flower petals to their neighbour (**Fig.7**).

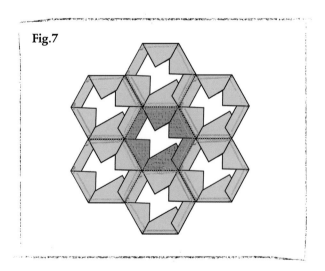

Fig.7

3 Repeat this process with all of the centres and the surrounding pieces. As they are done, lay under a heavy book as a way of flattening the shapes whilst you are sewing.

4 Now add a white surround to one flower, and gradually build up the pattern following **Fig.8**. This isn't a job that you will finish in a night, but if you keep working a little at a time, you will make good progress – and hand sewing is good for the soul!

5 Follow **Fig.8** for the design of the whole quilt – note where the half hexagons are used down the long edges to create a straight line.

6 As each hexagon becomes surrounded by other hexagons you can remove the paper or card from the project and also any visible tacking (basting) stitches. Press the quilt top using some clean cotton to cover the quilt. You will have bulk on the back from the excess seam allowance but this creates a nice cosy look.

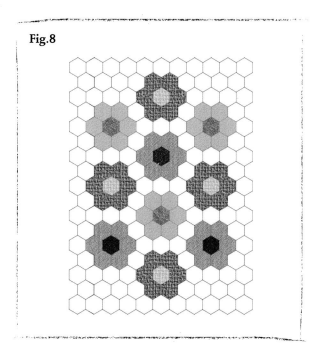

Fig.8

FINISHING OFF

1 Use a long ruler to straighten up the long edges and cut the points off the short edges as in **Fig.9**.

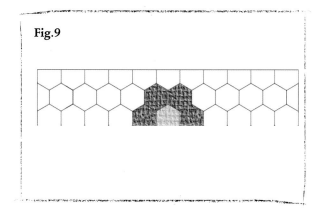

Fig.9

2 Cut a piece of wadding slightly bigger than the finished hexagon top. Pin through each central flower – smoothing the top out over the wadding.

3 Hand quilt the hexagon top to the wadding if you wish – I tend to use small running stitches in the ditch (invisibly in the seams) around each flower through the layers of the quilt (**Fig.10**).

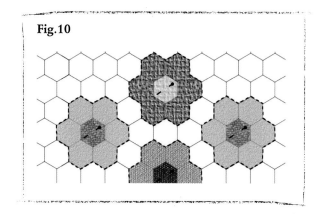

Fig.10

4 Once quilted, trim the wadding to be the same size as the quilt top, remove any remaining papers and tack (baste) the edges together.

5 Cut your cotton backing fabric to be the same size as the top. Lay the backing facing upwards and then the quilt top facing downwards, match the edges and sew starting at the lowest edge of the quilt, using a 0.5cm (¼in) seam allowance. Finish sewing about 6cm (2⅜in) away from your starting point (**Fig.11**).

6 Trim away excess seam allowance at corners and turn through to right side, pushing the corners out and rolling the seams to the outside of the quilt. Press flat. Close the opening with a slip stitch (see Hand Sewing Techniques: Slip Stitch).

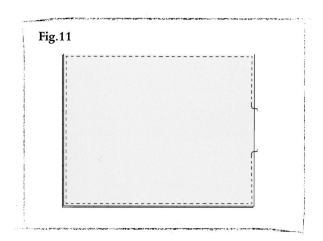

Fig.11

HOW TO
Sew
Luna AND friends

In this section we cover how to sew the animal bodies. Most of the process involves hand sewing, although there are parts that can be completed on a machine. You will find that Luna and Wilhelmina follow the same body construction, although their heads and tails differ.

Reynard, Freddie and Clementine all have a different body construction but their heads and tails are individual to each one. The animals are roughly 40.6cm (16in) tall when finished, but can wear any of the outfits in this book or that have been designed for Luna.

How to Make Luna

YOU WILL NEED

- **23cm (9in) x 92cm (36¼in) light grey felt**
- **15cm (6in) x 20cm (8in) cotton lawn fabric**
- **12.5cm (5in) x 12.5cm (5in) mid-weight fusible interfacing**
- **Two 10mm (³⁄₈in) buttons for eyes and two 15mm (⁵⁄₈in) buttons for arm joints**
- **Wool yarn for tail (optional)**
- **Toy stuffing about 120gm (4½oz)**
- **Six-stranded embroidery cotton (floss) in brown for facial features**
- **Basic sewing kit (see Materials)**

Use a 0.5cm (¼in) seam allowance, unless a different amount is stated.

CUTTING OUT

1 Cut around your paper pattern pieces carefully using scissors. I like to cut along the outside of the black line.

2 Pin the pattern pieces onto the felt using the layout in **Fig.1** as a guide. Mark any notches/triangles with a tiny snip in the felt. Unpin your pattern pieces. Cut out a pair of ears and a pair of footpads from the lawn fabric. Cut out a pair of ears from interfacing. Mark the notches as before. Transfer all other pattern markings using tailor's tacks or a water-soluble pen.

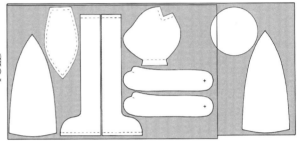

Fig.1

MAKING UP

Making the Ears:

1 Using an iron, fuse the interfacing to the wrong side of the print ears. Place the right side of a print ear onto one felt ear, matching edges and sew around the two edges, leaving the bottom open (**Fig.2**). You can machine sew or use a backstitch (see Hand Sewing Stitches: Backstitch). Repeat to make the second ear.

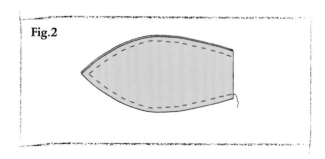

Fig.2

2 Trim the seam allowance off at the points and then turn each ear through to the right side. Use a knitting needle or similar tool to carefully push the shape out. Roll the seams out to the edge between your fingers and press flat with a warm iron.

3 Sew through the ear layers to hold them together on a central line, trying to keep your stitches invisible on the felt side. Finish about two-thirds of the way up. Fold each ear in half lengthways, enclosing the print fabric (**Fig.3**), and pin in place.

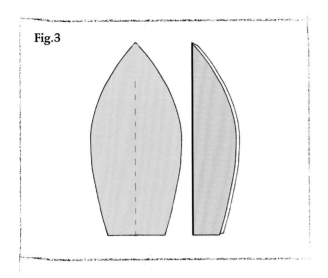

Fig.3

Making the Head:

1 Line up the bottom of an ear with the straight edge of a head piece, making sure the open (printed) edges of the ear are facing the nose. Fold the head piece over to cover the ear as in **Fig.4**. Make sure that the ear is tucked right up to the fold point. Sew through all layers on the marked sewing line. Use a backstitch or sewing machine for this stage. Repeat this step with the other ear and the other head piece, but make sure it is all the opposite way to the first one.

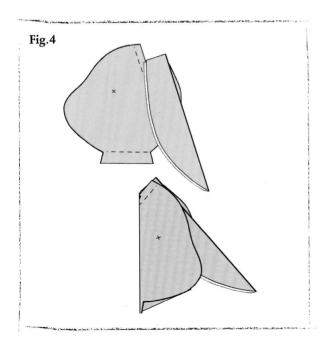

Fig.4

2 Turn the head pieces out to the right side and pin the centre front seams together so that the edges are level and the ear seams match up. Oversew the two pieces together, leaving the neck opening free (**Fig.5**).

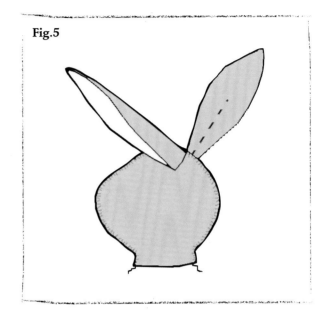

Fig.5

3 Stuff the head through the neck opening using small pieces of stuffing to build up the shape (**Fig.6**). Tuck the neck seam allowance up into the head.

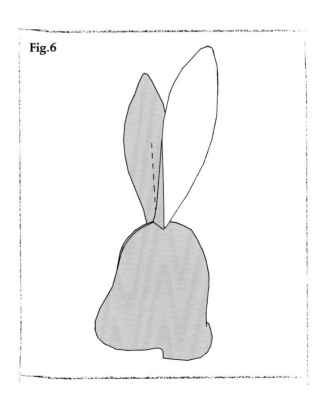

Fig.6

Making the Legs:

1 Oversew two leg pieces together down the long back seam. Starting from the foot, sew the front seam up to just over the foot (**Fig.7**).

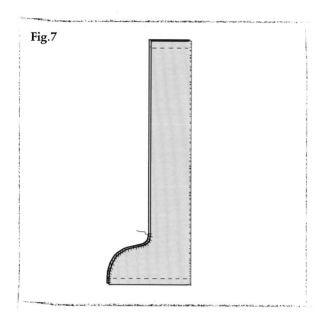

Fig.7

2 Now turn the leg so that these seams are to the inside and pin the footpad in place, using the notches on the footpad to match up with the seams you have just sewn. Ease the footpad in place and sew all the way around using a backstitch (**Fig.8**). Turn the foot back to be right side out with the raw edges enclosed and stuff the foot firmly. Resume oversewing the front leg seam, stuffing the leg firmly as you go. When you have completed one leg, repeat for the other leg. Leave about 1cm (⅜in) at the top with no stuffing. The legs should be the firmest stuffed part of the bunny (and the same length). At the top, fold each leg so that the front and back seams are in line with one another to close the opening and either pin or sew together.

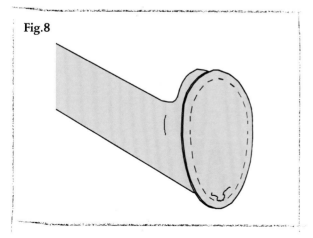

Fig.8

Making the Body:

1 Take two of the body pieces and oversew down one edge. Sew the third body piece onto another free side, and then join the remaining two free edges together, starting at the lower edge of the body and finishing after about 5cm (2in) before fastening off (**Fig.9**). Turn inside out, so that the seams are to the inside ready for the next stage.

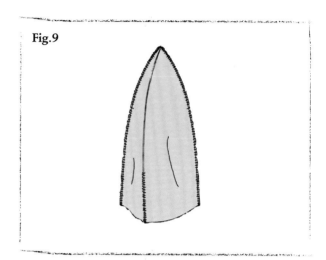

Fig.9

2 Push the legs inside the turned body. Feed them in through the opening in the body seam left in the previous step. Position the flattened top of each leg level with one of the lower edges of the body so that the outside edge of each flattened leg is in line with a tummy seam and the toes are facing up towards the tummy. Sew in place using a backstitch or tacking (basting) stitch (**Fig.10**).

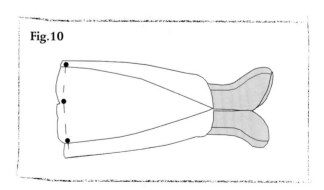

Fig.10

3 Take the circular base and matching up the three notches to the three seams of the body, enclose the raw edges of the legs and using a backstitch sew through all layers of the tummy, legs and base (**Fig.11**). A double thread is better when sewing through four thicknesses of felt. Complete the sewing around the circle.

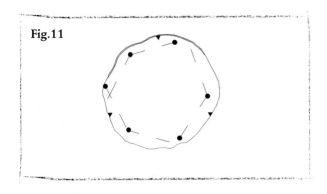

Fig.11

4 Turn the body back out so that the legs are dangling. Stuff the body and sew down the opening, starting from the top and meeting up with where you had previously sewn. Make sure that you use enough stuffing for the body to be firm.

5 Check you have enough stuffing in the head, but still a gap for the point of the body cone. Push the point of the body cone into the head. Using a medium-size darner needle and double thread, sew the head to the body using a slip stitch and ensuring it is well attached by going around the neck at least twice (**Fig.12**).

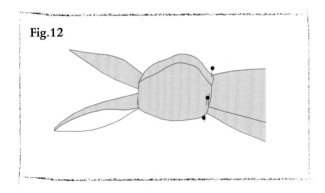

Fig.12

Making the Arms:

1 Match two arm pieces and sew together starting at the back of the arm. Oversew over the arm top, down the front and down to the hand (**Fig.13**). Use a deeper stitch to define the thumb and then oversew until you are 4cm (1½in) away from where you started.

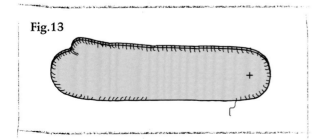

Fig.13

2 Stuff the arm firmly and then close the opening. Repeat this process to make a second arm.

3 Stitch the arms onto the body so that the top of the arm matches the level of the neck seam. Check you have the thumbs facing forwards. Position the buttons on the arms using the pattern piece as a guide. Use a double thread and the darner to sew the arms onto the body, going through the whole body and passing through the buttons on each side (**Fig.14**). Don't pull the arms in so tight that they change the shape of the body, but just enough to pull the arms in snug to the body. Secure by passing the needle through at least fifteen times – this needs to be secure as you will be moving the arms frequently to dress Luna and Wilhelmina.

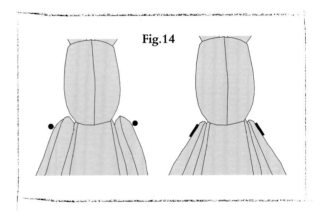

Fig.14

FINISHING OFF

1 Using three strands of brown embroidery thread, sew on buttons for eyes in a similar way to the arms, checking the pattern piece for positioning. Add the eyes at the same time, sewing through the face, but this time pulling the eyes in slightly to indent the face a little.

2 Use three strands of embroidery thread to satin stitch a triangular nose (see Hand Sewing Stitches: Satin Stitch). The top of the nose should measure 6.5cm (2½in) from the ear/head seam. The nose should be about 1cm (⅜in) wide at its widest point.

3 Adding a tail is optional. Using the wool, make a pompom for the tail by winding the wool around a credit card or piece of stiff card. Snip down both edges and bind the centre with a remnant of wool. Shape and fluff up the wool and then trim with a pair of scissors to be about 2cm (¾in) in diameter. Sew the tail onto the back seam of the body just above the base. Your bunny is now ready to be loved and dressed.

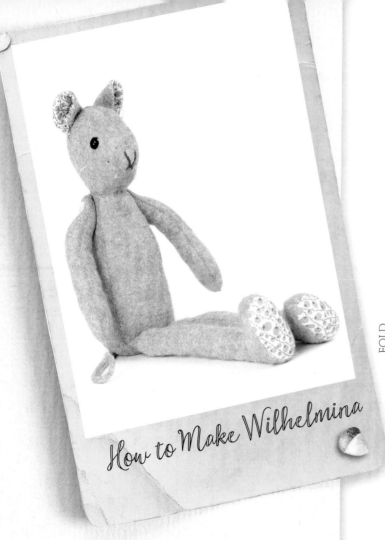

How to Make Wilhelmina

YOU WILL NEED

- **23cm (9in) x 92cm (36¼in) hazelnut felt**
- **15cm (6in) x 20cm (8in) cotton lawn fabric**
- **Two 10mm (⅜in) buttons for eyes and two 15mm (⅝in) buttons for arm joints**
- **Toy stuffing about 120gm (4½oz)**
- **1m (39½in) of 0.8mm elastic cord**
- **Six-stranded embroidery cotton (floss) in brown and pink for facial features**
- **Basic sewing kit (see Materials)**

Use a 0.5cm (¼in) seam allowance, unless a different amount is stated.

CUTTING OUT

1 Cut around your paper pattern pieces carefully using scissors. I like to cut along the outside of the black line.

2 Pin the pattern pieces onto the felt using the layout in **Fig.1** as a guide. Mark any notches/triangles with a tiny snip in the felt. Unpin your pattern pieces. Cut out a pair of ears and a pair of footpads from the lawn fabric. Mark the notches as before. Transfer all other pattern markings using tailor's tacks or a water-soluble pen.

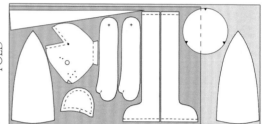

FOLD

Fig.1

MAKING UP

Making the Ears:
1 Taking a felt ear piece and a print ear piece, with right sides together, match up the edges and sew around the curved edges leaving the bottom notched edge open. You can machine sew or use a hand sewn backstitch (see Hand Sewing Stitches: Backstitch). Repeat to make the second ear, making sure it is a mirror image to the first (**Fig.2**).

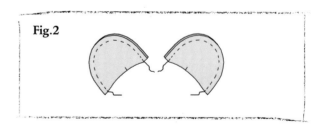

Fig.2

2 Trim the seam allowance down to 0.25cm (⅛in) and then turn through to the right side. Roll the seams out to the edge between your fingers and press flat with a warm iron.

3 Fold the shorter end of the ear over at the notch so that the lining is to the inside and so the lower edges match up. Repeat with the other ear so it is a mirror image. Tack (baste) across the lower edge to keep in place (**Fig.3**).

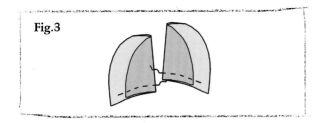

Fig.3

Making the Head:

1 Follow the instructions in How to Make Luna for how to sew Wilhelmina's head but make sure when you position the ears on the head that the folded section of the ear is towards the top of the head and touching the head (**Fig.4**).

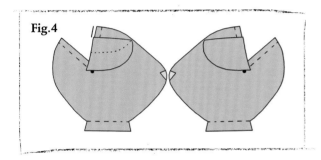

Fig.4

Sewing the Whiskers:

1 Cut a piece of elastic cord – about 50cm (19¾in). Using a large needle, thread the elastic onto the needle and knot the long end. (You might need to cut the end of the elastic at an angle to get it through the eye.) If you wish (but it's possible without) move the stuffing away from the felt and insert the needle up inside the head and bring out at one of the marked whisker positions. Pull through and trim.

2 Using the same elastic, repeat the previous step for the other whiskers. Use the remaining elastic as necessary – the whiskers can be trimmed to between 4cm – 5cm (1½in–2in). Do it gradually until you are happy (**Fig.5**).

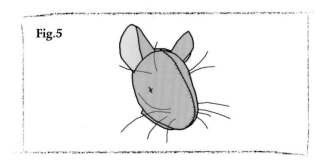

Fig.5

3 If you wish to, use a soft pencil to make a darker mark around the whisker position.

Making the Tail:

1 The tail pattern is a skinny triangle. Start rolling the felt onto itself at the widest end and pin the free edge down onto the bulk of the roll and continue to work your way down the tail: rolling, flattening and pinning (**Fig.6**).

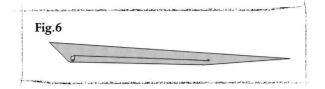

Fig.6

2 When you get to the narrowest end it will become impossible to wrap the tail onto anything, so trim the tail down to a point that you are able to pin down. Sew using a slip stitch (see Hand Sewing Stitches: Slip Stitch), attaching the pinned edge to the bulky roll.

3 When this is completed, starting at the thinner edge use a long backstitch along the seam, pulling tight with every stitch so the tail starts curling up. Continue until you feel the tail is right and then fasten off securely (**Fig.7**).

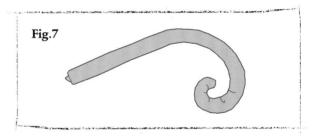

Fig.7

Making the Legs, Body and Arms:

1 Follow the instructions in How to Make Luna for how to sew Wilhelmina's legs, body and arms, placing the fatter end of Wilhelmina's tail against the back body seam at the same time that the legs are attached to the body.

FINISHING OFF

1 Using three strands of brown embroidery thread, sew on buttons for eyes in a similar way to the arms, checking the pattern piece for positioning. Add the eyes at the same time, sewing through the face, but this time pulling the eyes in slightly to indent the face a little.

2 Use embroidery thread to satin stitch a nose on (see Hand Sewing Stitches: Satin Stitch). The level marked on the pattern is for the highest nose point. We used three strands of a dark brown to create a cross shape, which is then caught at the point the lines meet. We then filled in the upper V with a soft pink using all six strands. Afterwards go over the brown outline lines again. The nose should be about 1cm (⅜in) wide at its widest point.

3 Alternatively, cut a felt triangle out and sew onto the face with tiny invisible stitches.

How to Make Reynard

YOU WILL NEED

- **22cm (8¾in) x 92cm (36¼in) ember felt**
- **18cm (7in) x 23cm (9in) snow white felt**
- **Two 10mm (³⁄₈in) buttons for eyes and three 15mm (⁵⁄₈in) buttons for arm joints and tail**
- **Toy stuffing about 120gm (4½oz)**
- **Six-stranded embroidery cotton (floss) in black for facial details**
- **Two 20mm (¾in) covering buttons (push the components together before you start)**
- **0.5m (19¾in) of 0.8mm elastic thread**
- **Basic sewing kit (see Materials)**

Use a 0.5cm (¼in) seam allowance, unless a different amount is stated.

CUTTING OUT

1 Cut around your paper pattern pieces carefully using scissors. I like to cut along the outside of the black line.

2 Pin the pattern pieces onto the felt using the layout in **Fig.1** as a guide and noting which pieces should be cut in which colour. The layout in **Fig.1** shows the ember felt folded in half with short ends together. You have plenty of white felt for the remaining pieces to go on in whichever way you choose. IMPORTANT: You must cut along the ear lines shown on the head pattern. Mark any notches/triangles with a tiny snip in the felt. Transfer all other pattern markings using tailor's tacks or a water-soluble pen.

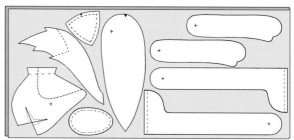

Fig.1

MAKING UP

Making the Ears:

1 Match up one white ear piece with one ember ear piece and sew around two edges, leaving the bottom (notched) edge open. You can either use a sewing machine to make this seam or use a backstitch (see Hand Sewing Stitches: Backstitch). Repeat to make the second ear making sure they are mirrored (**Fig.2**).

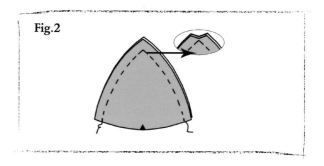

Fig.2

2 Trim the seam allowance off at the points and turn through to the right side. Use a knitting needle or similar to help push the shape out. Press flat with a warm iron.

Making the Head:

1 Working with one head piece at a time, lay the contrast white felt jaw piece so it sits over the head piece. Oversew in place along the curved seam. Once this is secure, you can cut away the extra ember coloured felt from underneath. Repeat with other pieces making sure you end up with two heads that are facing opposite ways (**Fig.3**).

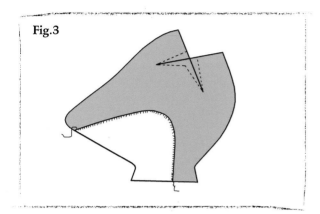

Fig.3

2 Lay the head pieces facing upwards and side by side with noses pointing outwards. Working with just one head piece at a time, place an ear with the white side down onto the right side of the head. Position the ear open edge along the cut line closest to the nose and 0.5cm (¼in) up from the cut line (**Fig.4**).

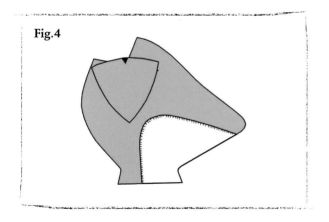

Fig.4

3 Fold the upper edge of the head back over the ear so that the ear is enclosed in the cut line as in **Fig.5**. Sew along the ear edge from the level of the notch to the end of the ear, catching in the head felt.

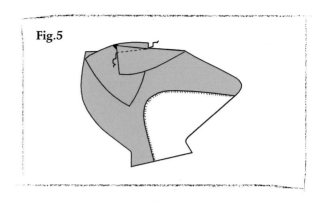

Fig.5

4 Bring the remaining ear edge around to match the remaining cut edge in the head, so that the ear edge sits in the end of the cut, and 0.5cm (¼in) above the cut edge as in **Fig.6**.

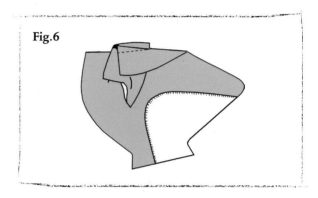

Fig.6

5 Sew in place. If you are confident, you can do all the positioning, folding and sewing of these two stages in one (**Fig.7**).

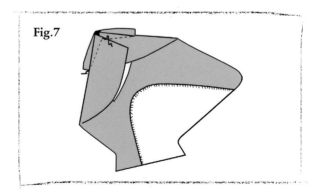

Fig.7

6 Repeat these steps with the other head piece and other ear, making sure it is facing the opposite way to the first head piece.

7 Turn the head pieces to be right side out and, working one side at a time, oversew the central seam together above the ears (**Fig.8**).

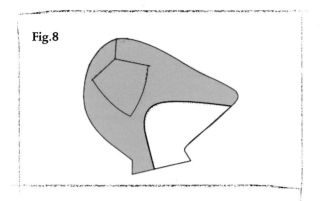

Fig.8

8 Now pin the head pieces together so that the edges match. Oversew the two pieces together, leaving the neck open. You may want to switch colour for the under nose sewing (**Fig.9**).

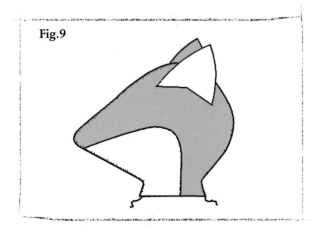

Fig.9

9 Stuff the head through the neck opening using small pieces of stuffing to build up the shape. Tuck the neck seam allowance up into the head.

Making the Body:
1 Take the two ember coloured body pieces and sew down the back seam, starting at the top point and sewing approximately 4cm (1½in), then fastening off. Resume sewing again leaving an opening of 6cm (2⅜in) and sew until you reach the snip or notch at the base (**Fig.10**).

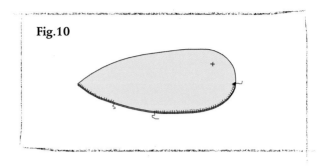

Fig.10

2 Now take the white tummy panel and pin one edge to one of the back pieces and sew all the way from the point to where the notches meet. Repeat along the remaining tummy/ back seam from the point to the notch (**Fig.11**).

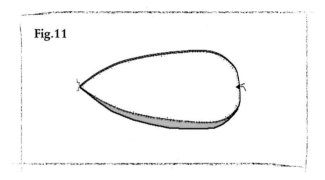

Fig.11

3 Stuff the body through the opening in the back seam of the body. When you are happy with the body shape close the back opening with oversewing.

4 Check you have enough stuffing in the head, but still a gap for the point of the cone to go in. Push the point of the body cone into the head. Pin to secure position.

5 Using a large needle and double thread sew the head to the body using a slip stitch and ensuring it is well attached by going around the neck at least twice.

Making the Legs:
1 Oversew two leg pieces together along the long back seam, starting at the foot and finishing about 7cm (2¾in) past the curve at the top. Then starting from the foot, sew the front seam up to just over the foot (**Fig.12**).

Fig.12

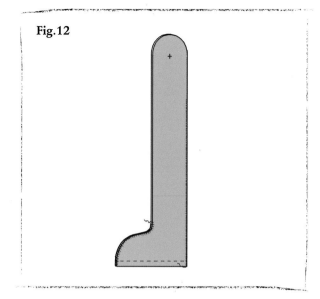

Fig.14

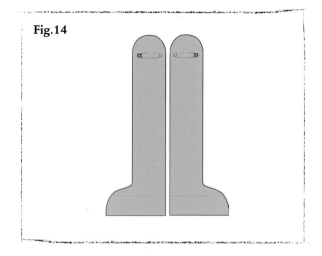

2 Now turn the leg so that these seams are to the inside and pin the footpad in place matching the notches on the footpad with the seams you have just sewn. Ease the footpad in and sew all the way around using a backstitch (**Fig.13**).

Fig.13

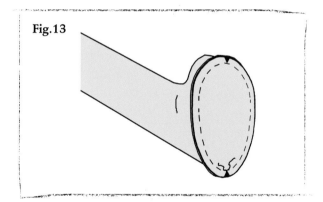

3 Turn the foot back out so that the raw edges of the felt are enclosed and stuff the foot firmly. Resume oversewing the front leg seam, stuffing the leg firmly as you go. Now stuff the top curve of the leg but before you make it too full, push a covered button inside the stuffed leg so that the shank part is facing the felt, and the domed part is resting against some stuffing. The shank should be about 1.5cm (⅝in) down from the highest part of the leg (roughly where the X is marked on the pattern). Use a safety pin on the outside of the felt to secure the shank in place (**Fig.14**).

4 Continue to stuff until firm and finish sewing all the way around. Repeat with other leg, but making sure that the shank is facing inwards to make an opposite leg.

5 Thread a large needle with elastic thread. Cut the end of the elastic at an angle to create a pointed end to go through the needle eye when threading. Pull the ends through so they are equal. Pass the threaded needle through the shank of the covered button in one leg (remove the safety pin). Push the needle through the body at the cross so that it comes out at the same position on the other side. You will have to compress the body so the needle comes out the other side. Pass the needle through the shank of the covered button on the other leg and then pass the needle through the body again to the first side. Finally go through the shank of the first leg again (**Fig.15**).

Fig.15

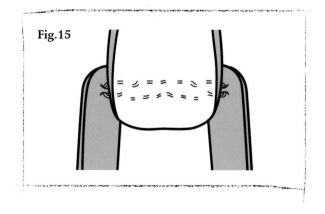

6 Pull both ends of elastic firmly/steadily to draw the legs into the body. When there is enough tension to pull the body in and make the leg tops seem to sit in sockets, knot the ends of the elastic together at least three times. Check everything is secure and trim the elastic closely so that the ends disappear between the leg and the body.

Making the Arms:

Follow the instructions in How to Make Luna for how to sew Reynard's arms.

Making the Tail:

1 Working with one tail piece at a time, lay the contrast tail tip over the main piece. Oversew in place along the inner seam. Once this is secure, you can cut away the extra ember coloured felt from underneath. Make sure you end up with two tails that are facing opposite ways (**Fig.16**).

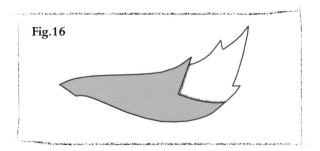

Fig.16

2 Match up the two tail pieces with wrong sides together and oversew all the way around leaving a gap on the under tail of about 6cm (2⅜in) to be able to stuff (**Fig.17**). Remember you can switch thread colour when you are sewing around the tail tip. Stuff the tail gently – so it isn't too full or heavy. Close the opening with oversewing once you are happy.

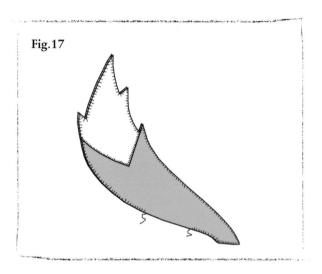

Fig.17

FINISHING OFF

1 Using black embroidery thread, sew on buttons for eyes in a similar way to the arms, checking your pattern piece for positioning. Add the eyes at the same time, sewing through the face, but this time just pulling the eyes in slightly to indent the face slightly.

2 Flatten the tip of the nose out and bend 1cm (⅜in) over and sew down to the seam below it, and use this triangular shape to embroider the nose with a satin stitch (see Hand Sewing Stitches: Satin Stitch).

3 To attach the tail (it is detachable so that if you want to make trousers for the fox you can put them on), sew a button onto the back body seam, about 6cm (2⅜in) up from the seam intersection on the fox's bottom. Take the tail and press the narrow top end flat so that the seam is running through the middle. Make a buttonhole either by hand or on a machine, cut open and button onto your fox. The buttonhole should be the same size as the button diameter (felt does give a bit so better to be tighter). If you never, ever want your fox to wear clothes you could sew the tail in the back seam in the Making the Body step.

How to Make Freddie

YOU WILL NEED

- **18cm (7in) x 91.5cm (36in) grey felt**
- **12.5cm (5in) square of black felt**
- **18cm (7in) x 23cm (9in) white felt**
- **Two 10mm (³⁄₈in) buttons for eyes and two 15mm (⁵⁄₈in) buttons for arm joints**
- **Toy stuffing about 140gm (5oz)**
- **Two 20mm (³⁄₄in) diameter covering buttons (push the components together before you start)**
- **0.5m (19³⁄₄in) of 0.8mm elastic thread**
- **You might also want to use a plastic nose – this should be 2cm (³⁄₄in) wide.**
- **Basic sewing kit (see Materials)**

Use a 0.5cm (¼in) seam allowance, unless a different amount is stated.

CUTTING OUT

1 Cut around your paper pattern pieces carefully using scissors. I like to cut along the outside of the black line.

2 Pin the pattern pieces onto the felt using the layout in **Fig.1** as a guide and noting which pieces should be cut in which colour. The layout in **Fig.1** shows the grey felt. You have plenty of black and white felt for the other pieces to go on whichever way you choose but remember to cut the head on the fold of the white felt. Cut the pieces out and mark any notches/triangles with a tiny snip in the felt. Transfer all other pattern markings using tailor's tacks or a water-soluble pen.

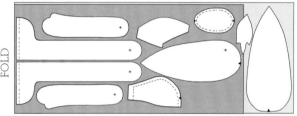

FOLD

Fig.1

MAKING UP

Making the Ears:
1 Match up one white ear piece with one black ear piece and sew around two edges, leaving the bottom (notched) edge open. You can either use a sewing machine or a backstitch (see Hand Sewing Stitches: Backstitch). Repeat to make the second ear (**Fig.2**).

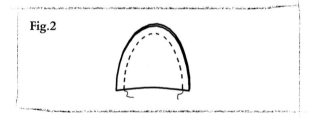

Fig.2

2 Turn ears through to the right side. Stretch the lower edge of the white felt a little. Pleat about 1cm (³⁄₈in) out of the width on the free edge of the black felt, therefore making the bottom edge of the black smaller, and pin. Roll the edges of the ear so that you can see a tip of white felt all the way around (**Fig.3**).

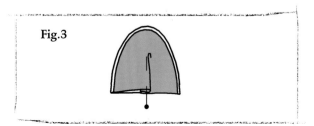

Fig.3

3 If the black felt edge is sitting longer at the bottom, trim back to the level of the white.

4 Press flat with a warm iron.

Making the Head:

1 Take the head piece and position the two contrast lower jaw pieces over the head piece. Oversew in place along the curved seam and the short end. Once this is secure, you can cut away the extra white felt from underneath, about 0.5cm (¼in) from the sewing line (**Fig.4**).

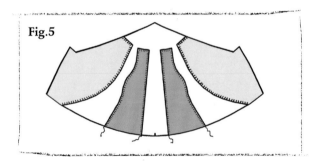

Fig.4

2 Position the two black eye stripes onto the head between the notches for the ears, using the markings you transferred from the pattern. Oversew around each shape. Don't cut away any felt from the back, as you did in previous step (**Fig.5**).

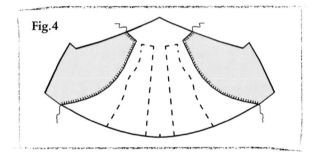

Fig.5

3 Lay the head piece facing upwards. Place ears with the black side down onto the head and so that the ears sit centrally over the black eye stripes. Tack (baste) in place (**Fig.6**).

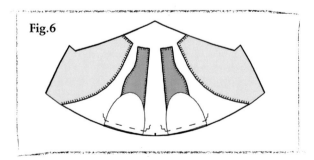

Fig.6

4 With right sides to the outside, fold the head in half matching the jaw edges and oversew the two sides together. You may want to switch to tonal thread for the under nose sewing (**Fig.7**).

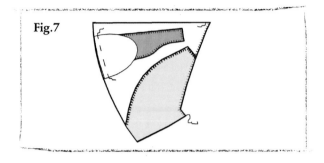

Fig.7

5 Prepare the nose by attaching a double thread onto the jaw seam 3cm (1¼in) down from the nose tip and then sew through the very end of the nose, flattening the top down so it folds over at the end. Secure your threads (**Fig.8**).

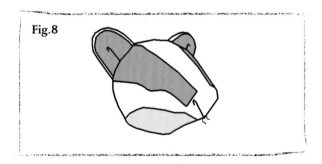

Fig.8

6 At this point decide whether you want a plastic or felt nose. For the felt nose go to step 11. For the plastic nose, make a small hole through the folded triangle with a bradawl or small scissors. Push the nose stalk through and pop the washer onto the other side. Adjust to be the right angle (**Fig.9**).

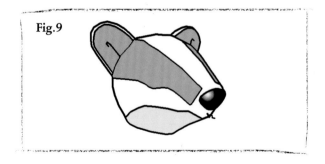

Fig.9

7 Match and sew the centre back seam of the back head pieces with wrong sides together, oversewing on the right side (**Fig.10**).

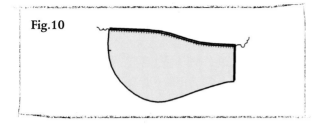

Fig.10

8 Push the front head inside out. With right sides together, match and pin the front head to the back head, ensuring the notches on the back head match at the ears on the front head. Sew together either with a machine or a hand backstitch. Machine sewing is easier here (**Fig.11**).

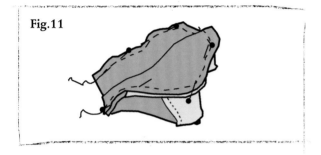

Fig.11

9 Staystitch around the neck edge, with short running stitches and double thread, about 0.5cm (¼in) up from the neck edge – this is to stop the neck stretching when you stuff it, so fasten off securely (**Fig.12**).

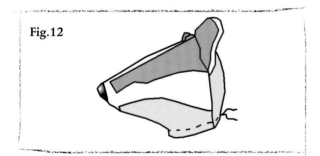

Fig.12

10 Stuff the head through the neck opening using small pieces of stuffing to build up the shape. Tuck the neck seam allowance up into the head.

11 If you have already attached a plastic nose, skip to Making the Body. To attach the felt nose, cut a 2.5cm (1in) square of black felt and fold in 0.5cm (¼in) along each edge. Starting along the top of the nose position on the head, place the folded edge so it sits on the ridge on the head and making sure it is central, sew in place with double black thread. Continue around the square making sure your seam allowances are tucked in (**Fig.13**). This technique creates a nice, chunky nose – but the needlework on it is a little tricky.

Fig.13

12 An easier option is to just sew on a square of felt about 1.25cm (½in) square without turning in the edges.

Making the Body:
1 Make Freddie's body and attach his head following the instructions for How to Make Reynard: Making the Body but ignoring the references to different coloured felt.

Making the Legs:
1 Follow the instructions in How to Make Reynard for how to make and attach Freddie's legs.

Making the Arms:
1 Follow the instructions in How to Make Luna for how to make and attach Freddie's arms.

Making the Tail:
1 Match up the two white tail pieces and sew all the way around, leaving a gap on one side to stuff lightly and then finish sewing up.

2 On one side add the contrast upper tail, positioning where you feel it looks best and oversew into position (**Fig.14**).

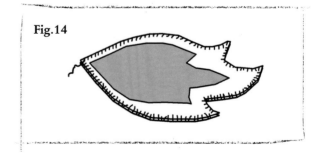

Fig.14

3 Oversew the tail to the back seam of the body with the top being about the height of the leg buttons.

FINISHING OFF

1 Using your head pattern piece for position, sew buttons on for eyes, sewing through the layers of felt.

How to Make Clementine

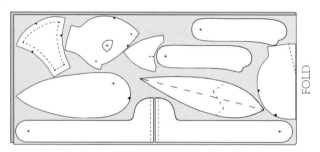

CUTTING OUT

1 Cut around your paper pattern pieces carefully using scissors. I like to cut along the outside of the black line.

2 Pin the pattern pieces for the main body onto the felt using the layout in **Fig.1** as a guide and noting which pieces should be cut in which colour. The layout in **Fig.1** shows the marmalade felt folded in half with short ends together.

FOLD

Fig.1

3 You have plenty of the white felt for the other pieces to go on whichever way you choose. Cut pieces out. Mark the notches shown on the pattern with a TINY snip in the felt, APART FROM THE EAR NOTCH WHICH SHOULD BE AS LONG AS THE SNIP ON THE PATTERN.

4 Cut along the small lines on the contrast nose. Mark any dots on the head with a tailor's tack or a water-soluble pencil or poke through the felt with the tapestry needle to leave a fairly recognisable hole. Unpin your pattern pieces from the cut felt. Cut out a pair of ears and a pair of footpads from the print fabric. Mark the notches shown on the pattern, with a TINY snip in the fabric.

MAKING UP

Making and Attaching the Ears:

1 With right sides together, match up one print ear piece with one felt ear piece and sew around two edges, leaving the bottom (notched) edge open (**Fig.2**).

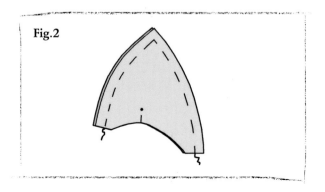

Fig.2

YOU WILL NEED

- **22cm (8¾in) x 92cm (36¼in) marmalade felt**
- **18cm (7in) x 23cm (9in) snow white felt**
- **25cm (10in) square of cotton lawn fabric**
- **Scrap of black felt**
- **Two buttons for eyes, two buttons for arm joints, one button for tail, all size 15mm (⅝in)**
- **Toy stuffing about 120gm (4½oz)**
- **Two 20mm (¾in) covering buttons (push the components together before you start)**
- **0.5m (19¾in) of 0.8mm elastic thread**
- **1m (39½in) of 1mm waxed cord for whiskers**
- **Basic sewing kit (see Materials)**

Use a 0.5cm (¼in) seam allowance, unless a different amount is stated.

2 Repeat to make the second ear – making sure they are opposite ways to one another. Trim the seam allowance off at the points, and then turn through to the right side.

3 Use a knitting needle or similar to help push the shape out. Press flat with a warm iron (**Fig.3**).

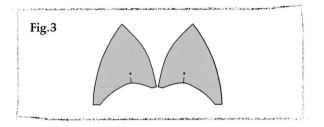

Fig.3

4 Line up the notch in one lower ear edge, with the tailor's tack on the upper front head piece, ensuring the print side is facing upwards. Tack (baste) in place. Repeat with other side (**Fig.4**).

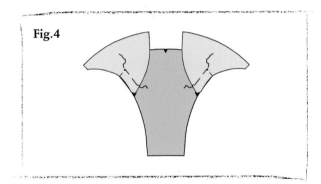

Fig.4

5 Take one side front head and match the tailor's tack to the notch on the ear and upper front, then pin and match down the front seam to the next set of tailor's tacks. Sew from the position of the tailor's tack to the lower tailor's tack using a 1cm (⅜in) seam allowance. In the diagram we've made this side front head panel semi-transparent to help you see the positioning (**Fig.5**).

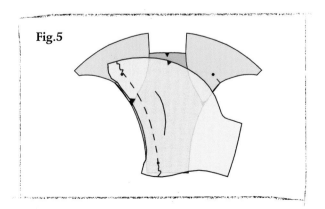

Fig.5

6 Repeat with the other side front head and the opposite side of the upper front head (**Fig.6**).

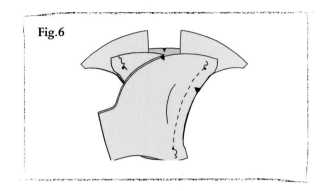

Fig.6

7 Press head seams open. Working one side at a time, open up the notch (long snip) in the ear and match the far end of the ear to the triangle notch in the side of the head. The ear's unsewn edge can just go straight across, rather than follow the curve of the outer head. Repeat with other side and tack (baste) in place (**Fig.7**).

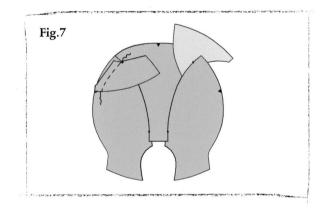

Fig.7

Making the Head:
1 With right sides together, make the back dart by folding the back head in half to match the two notches on the neckline and finger press along to the marked top of the dart. If you wish, draw a line to join these points. Pin in place and sew, following the drawn line from the edge of the neck to the point (**Fig.8**).

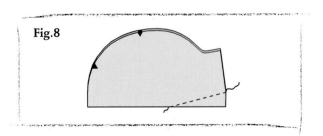

Fig.8

2 Attach the back head to the front with right sides together, match the lower neck of the back to the front at each side. Match the notches all the way around and sew using a 1cm (⅜in) seam allowance. You may wish to just sew up to the notch which corresponds with the centre of the ear. Then resume, when you have moved the bulk of the ear to the side, sew across the top of the head until you reach the other centre of ear. Move the bulk of the second ear out of the way and sew down to the other neck edge (**Fig.9**).

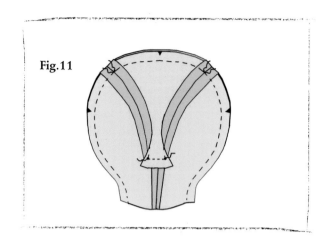

Fig.11

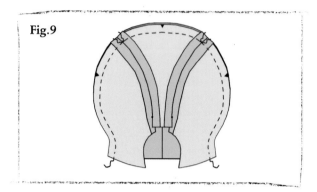

Fig.9

3 Match the two curved edges of the side fronts and sew together from the marked tailor's tack/previous stitching to the bottom edge. Be careful to keep the upper head out of the way of your seam (in our diagram it's shown tucked inside the head) (**Fig.10**).

5 Push the head through to be right sides out – you may have to stretch the neck a little. Give everything a bit of a stretch when it's turned through.

6 Stuff the head through the neck opening using small pieces of stuffing to build up the shape. Tuck the neck seam allowance up into the head.

7 Take the white nose backing piece and centre the top up over the upper head. The triangle point of the white piece should line up with the horizontal seam on the front head (**Fig.12**).

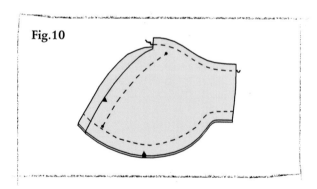

Fig.10

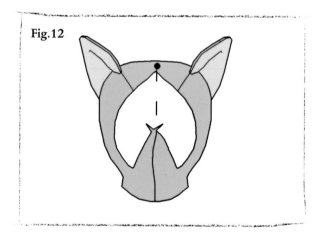

Fig.12

4 To finish the nose, flatten the upper head nose area against the seam of the lower face. Move the seam allowance of the side front seams out of the way and sew between the tailor's tack marks – which will be where your previous sewing lines finished (**Fig.11**).

8 Bring the edges of the contrast piece around so they match up with the centre seam on the lower head – each head will be stuffed differently so it might be that you need to overlap/trim a little off the length. Hand sew the nose backing piece onto the main head around the edge using white thread. Sew the lower edges of the nose piece to one another and sew down the triangle piece to lay flat against the head. Oversew all around the edge of the contrast piece to attach it to the head (**Fig.13**).

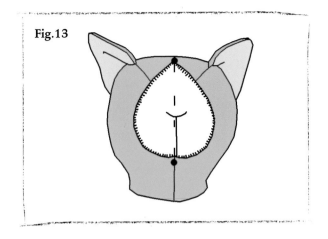

Fig.13

Making the Arms:

1 Follow the instructions in How to Make Luna for how to make and attach Clementine's arms.

Making the Tail:

1 Lay the white tail tip over the main tail piece. Oversew in place along the jagged edge (**Fig.15**). Once this is secure, you can cut away the extra contrast coloured felt from underneath. Now fold the whole tail in half and oversew the edges – leaving a stuffing gap. Remember you can switch to tonal thread when you are sewing on white.

2 Stuff the tail gently – so it isn't too full or heavy. Close the opening with oversewing once you are happy.

3 To attach the tail, sew onto the back of the body with a button, about 6cm (2⅜in) up from the seam intersection on the cat's bottom.

9 Use the pattern piece as a guideline and position then sew down the eye backing pieces. Sew buttons on for eyes in a similar way as you sew on the arms, checking your pattern piece for positioning. Sew on the small triangle of black felt for a nose (**Fig.14**).

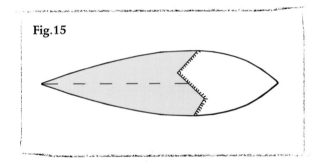

Fig.15

Fig.14

10 Using the thick cord and a tapestry needle, cut a piece of cord about 15cm (6in) long. Thread onto needle and knot one end. Move the stuffing away from the felt and insert the needle up inside the head and bring out at one of the marked positions for whiskers.

11 Pull through and repeat for the other whiskers.

12 If you wish to, use a soft pencil to make a darker mark around the whisker position.

Making the Body:

1 Make Clementine's body and attach her head following the instructions for How to Make Reynard: Making the Body but ignoring the references to different coloured felt.

Making the Legs:

1 Follow the instructions in How to Make Reynard for how to make and attach Clementine's legs.

The Patterns

The patterns for the projects are shown at full size. When using patterns follow these general guidelines:

- Refer to the pattern layout diagram with each project to see which patterns are needed.

- The patterns have seam allowances included. The allowances are stated in the project instructions.

- Before cutting, iron the patterns and your fabric to remove any creases.

- Once copied, cut your paper patterns out first before you pin them onto the fabric.

- Some patterns only show half of the shape and these are clearly marked. In these cases, place the marked line along the fold of the fabric, so when the shape is cut out you will double the pattern.

- Cutting out is crucial to success so the use of pins when positioning a pattern on fabric will really improve your results. When pinning, keep the entire pin inside the pattern so there is no danger of your scissors hitting the pin.

- Grainlines – placing your pattern pieces on the grainline of fabric helps the pattern pieces keep their shape. The grainline of a fabric is parallel to the selvedges – the finished edges of a piece of fabric. For these tiny garments try to follow our layouts as we have placed the shapes along the grainline, but on this scale of things it's not going to make or break your garment.

You will see symbols on the patterns – some of the common ones are shown and explained here.

 Fabric grain

– – – Sewing line

▼ ❙ ● Triangle/notch and dot position markers

—✕— Buttonhole and button positions

▼——▼ Place on fold of fabric

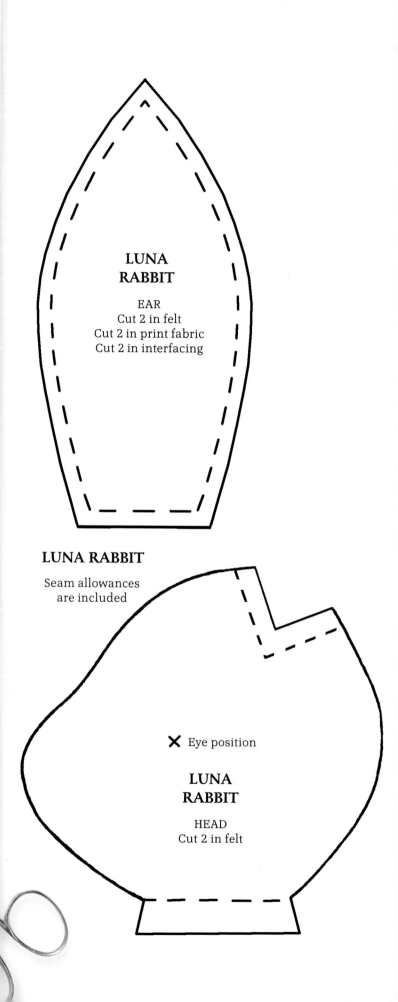

LUNA RABBIT

EAR
Cut 2 in felt
Cut 2 in print fabric
Cut 2 in interfacing

LUNA RABBIT

Seam allowances
are included

✕ Eye position

LUNA RABBIT

HEAD
Cut 2 in felt

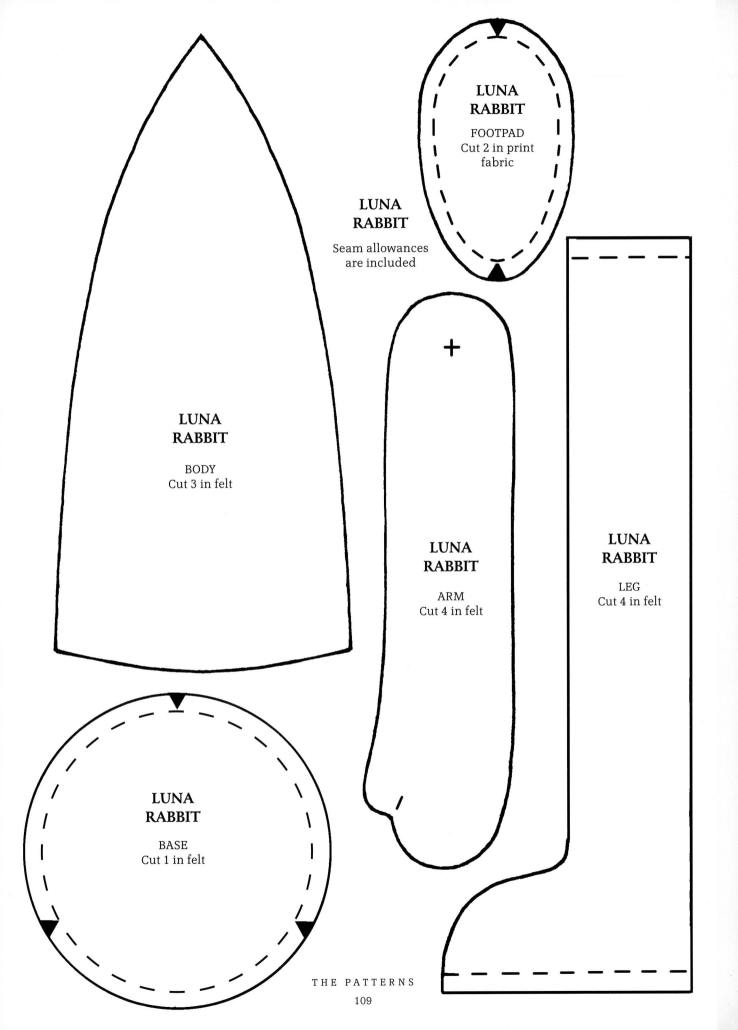

LUNA
RABBIT

FOOTPAD
Cut 2 in print
fabric

LUNA
RABBIT

Seam allowances
are included

LUNA
RABBIT

BODY
Cut 3 in felt

LUNA
RABBIT

ARM
Cut 4 in felt

LUNA
RABBIT

LEG
Cut 4 in felt

LUNA
RABBIT

BASE
Cut 1 in felt

THE PATTERNS

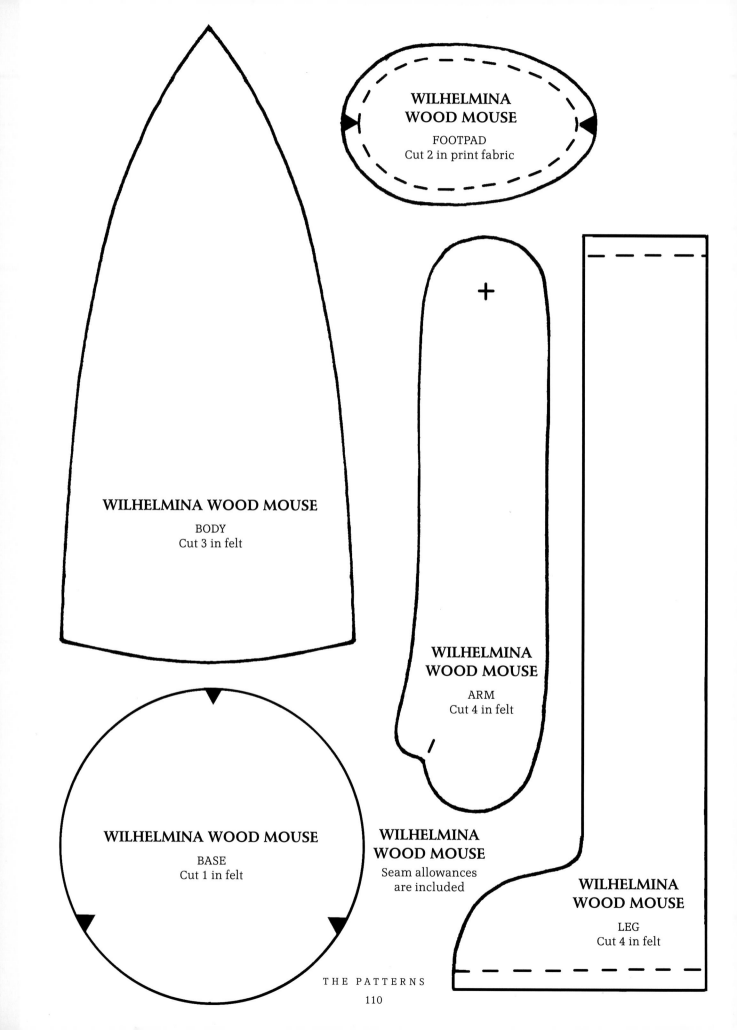

WILHELMINA WOOD MOUSE

FOOTPAD
Cut 2 in print fabric

WILHELMINA WOOD MOUSE

BODY
Cut 3 in felt

WILHELMINA WOOD MOUSE

ARM
Cut 4 in felt

WILHELMINA WOOD MOUSE

BASE
Cut 1 in felt

WILHELMINA WOOD MOUSE

Seam allowances
are included

WILHELMINA WOOD MOUSE

LEG
Cut 4 in felt

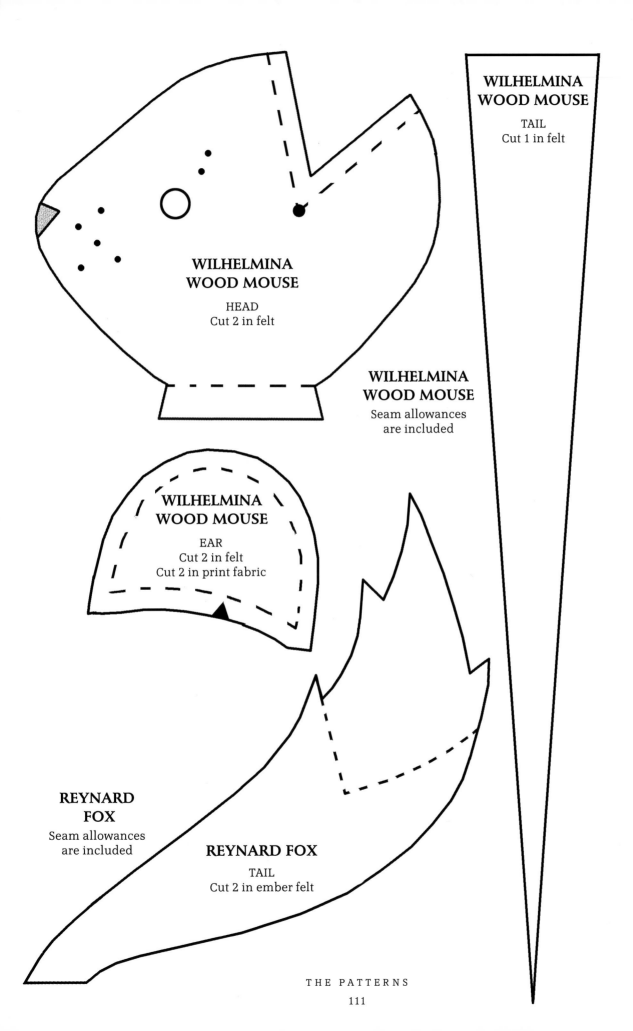

**WILHELMINA
WOOD MOUSE**

TAIL
Cut 1 in felt

**WILHELMINA
WOOD MOUSE**

HEAD
Cut 2 in felt

**WILHELMINA
WOOD MOUSE**

Seam allowances
are included

**WILHELMINA
WOOD MOUSE**

EAR
Cut 2 in felt
Cut 2 in print fabric

**REYNARD
FOX**

Seam allowances
are included

REYNARD FOX

TAIL
Cut 2 in ember felt

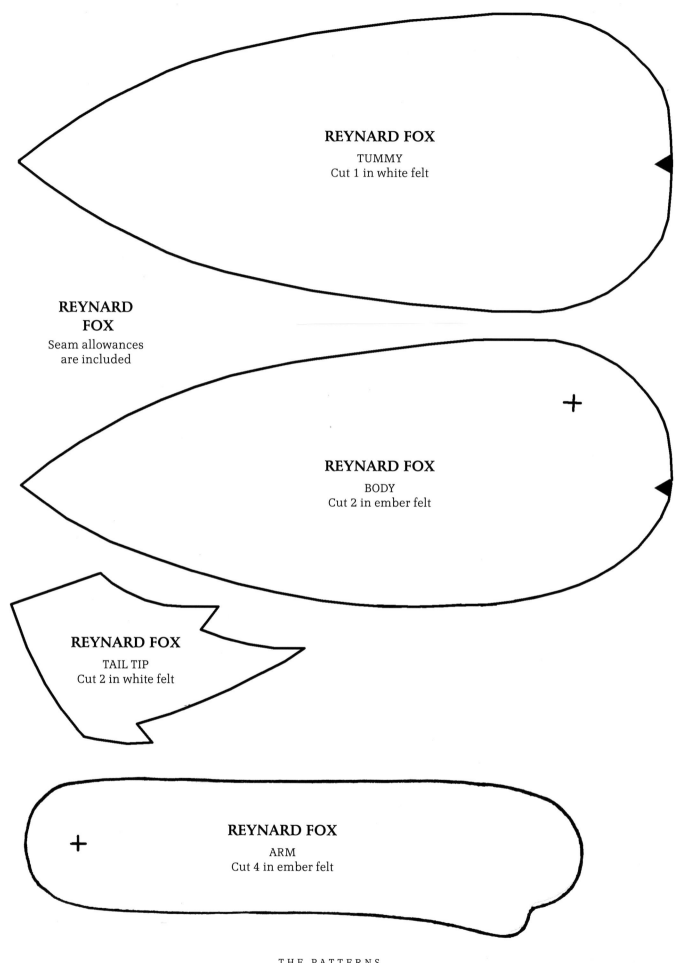

REYNARD FOX

TUMMY
Cut 1 in white felt

REYNARD FOX

Seam allowances
are included

REYNARD FOX

BODY
Cut 2 in ember felt

REYNARD FOX

TAIL TIP
Cut 2 in white felt

REYNARD FOX

ARM
Cut 4 in ember felt

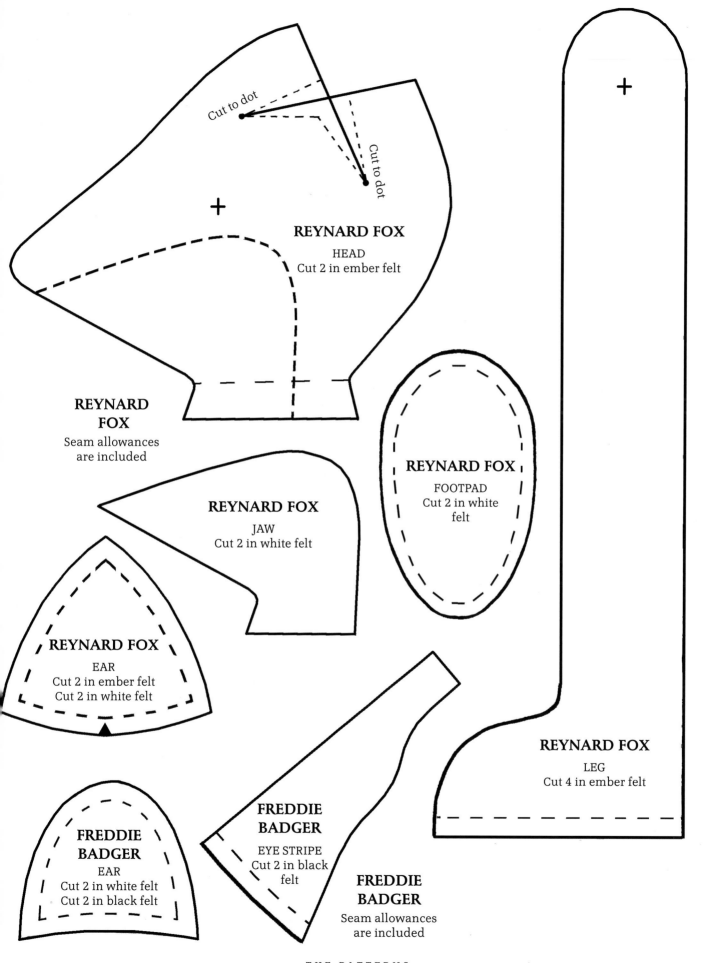

Cut to dot

Cut to dot

REYNARD FOX

HEAD
Cut 2 in ember felt

**REYNARD
FOX**

Seam allowances
are included

REYNARD FOX

JAW
Cut 2 in white felt

REYNARD FOX

FOOTPAD
Cut 2 in white
felt

REYNARD FOX

EAR
Cut 2 in ember felt
Cut 2 in white felt

REYNARD FOX

LEG
Cut 4 in ember felt

**FREDDIE
BADGER**

EAR
Cut 2 in white felt
Cut 2 in black felt

**FREDDIE
BADGER**

EYE STRIPE
Cut 2 in black
felt

**FREDDIE
BADGER**

Seam allowances
are included

THE PATTERNS

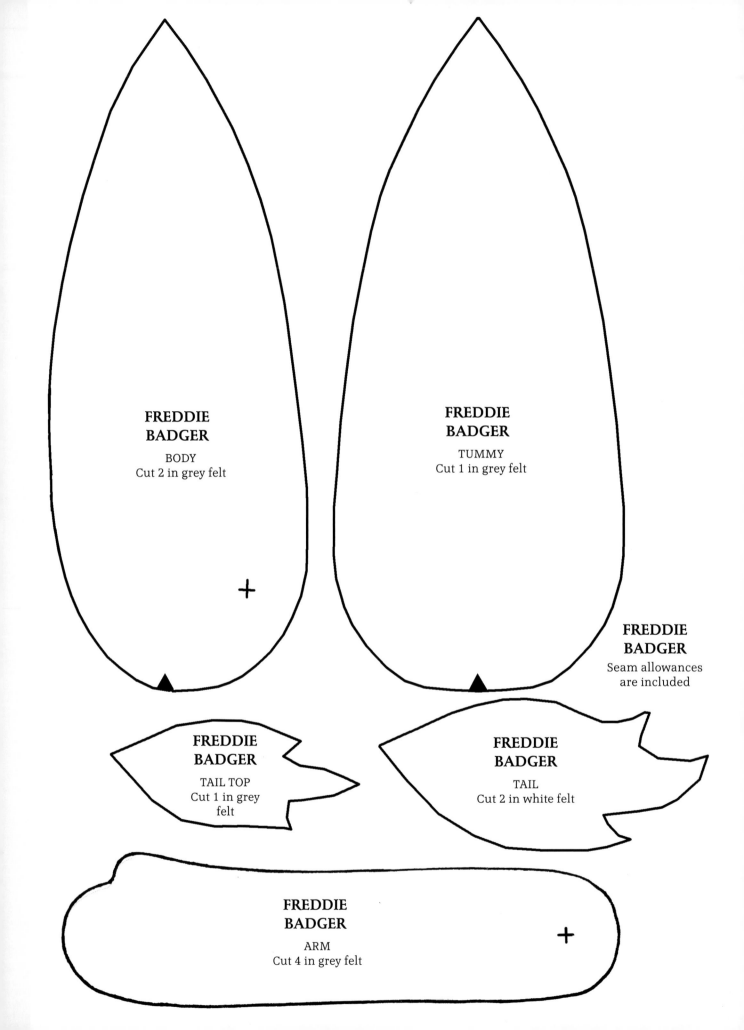

FREDDIE BADGER

BODY
Cut 2 in grey felt

FREDDIE BADGER

TUMMY
Cut 1 in grey felt

FREDDIE BADGER

Seam allowances are included

FREDDIE BADGER

TAIL TOP
Cut 1 in grey felt

FREDDIE BADGER

TAIL
Cut 2 in white felt

FREDDIE BADGER

ARM
Cut 4 in grey felt

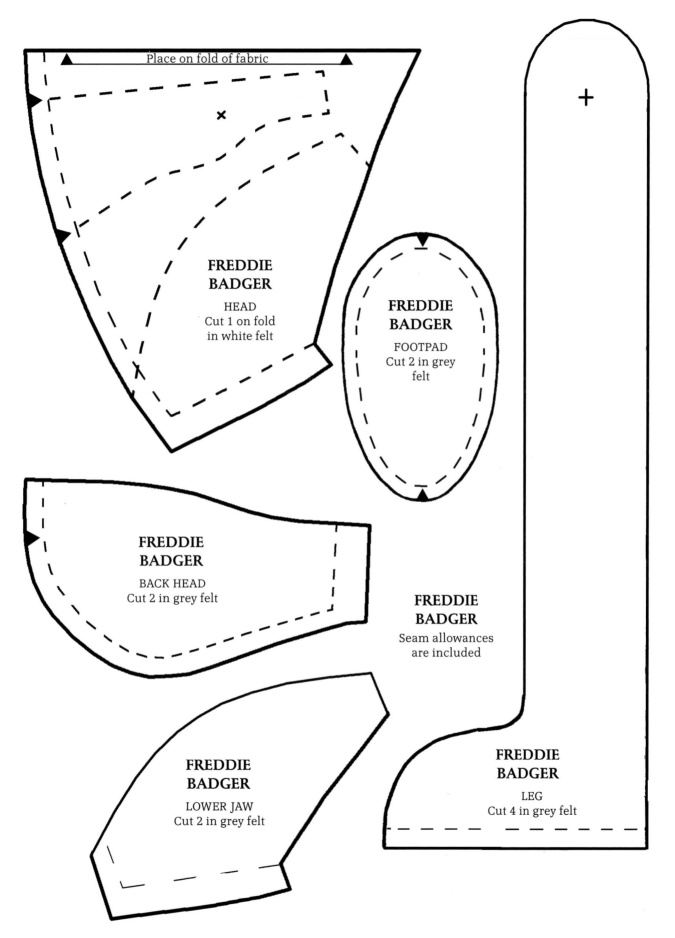

Place on fold of fabric

FREDDIE BADGER

HEAD
Cut 1 on fold
in white felt

FREDDIE BADGER

FOOTPAD
Cut 2 in grey felt

FREDDIE BADGER

BACK HEAD
Cut 2 in grey felt

FREDDIE BADGER

Seam allowances
are included

FREDDIE BADGER

LOWER JAW
Cut 2 in grey felt

FREDDIE BADGER

LEG
Cut 4 in grey felt

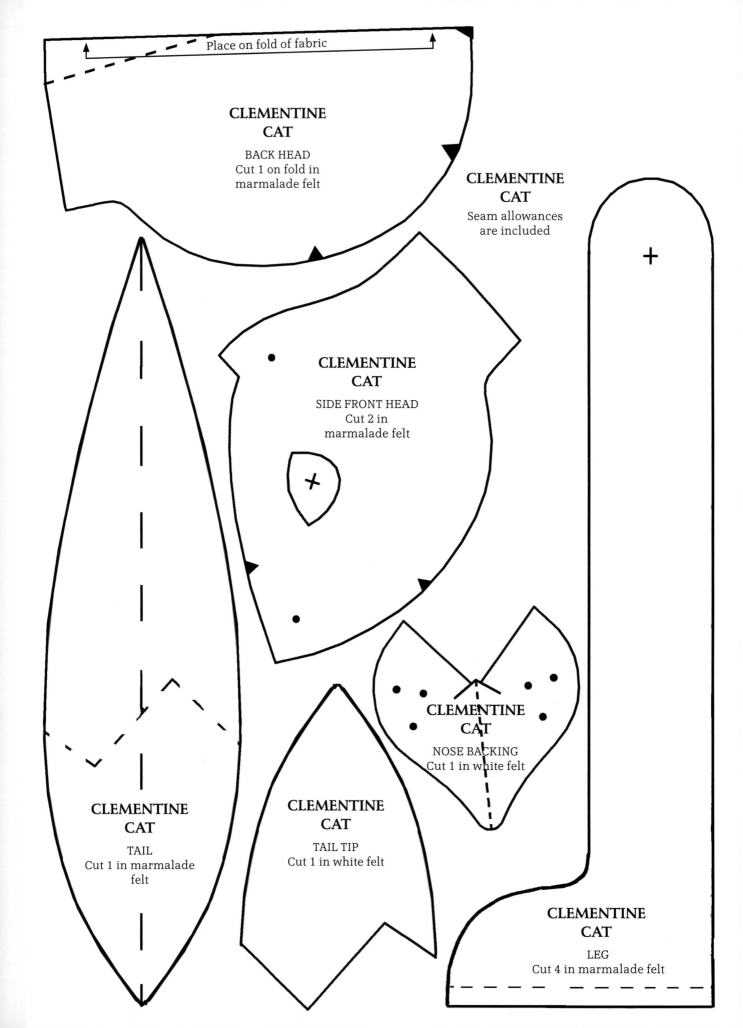

Place on fold of fabric

CLEMENTINE CAT

BACK HEAD
Cut 1 on fold in
marmalade felt

CLEMENTINE CAT

Seam allowances
are included

CLEMENTINE CAT

SIDE FRONT HEAD
Cut 2 in
marmalade felt

CLEMENTINE CAT

NOSE BACKING
Cut 1 in white felt

CLEMENTINE CAT

TAIL
Cut 1 in marmalade
felt

CLEMENTINE CAT

TAIL TIP
Cut 1 in white felt

CLEMENTINE CAT

LEG
Cut 4 in marmalade felt

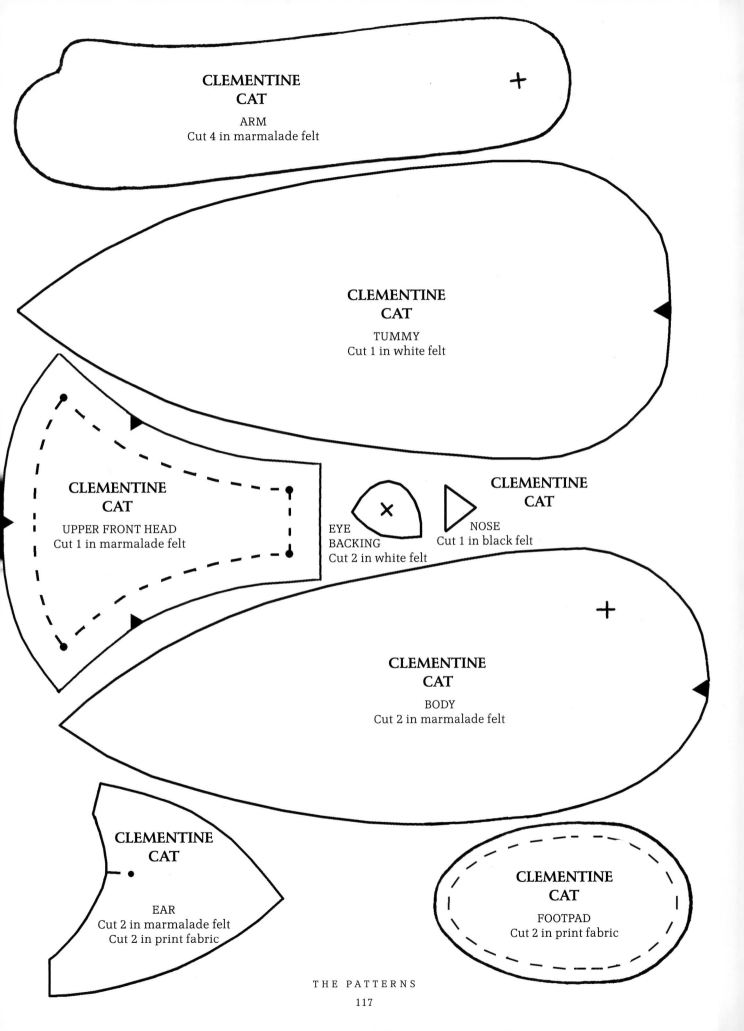

CLEMENTINE CAT

ARM
Cut 4 in marmalade felt

CLEMENTINE CAT

TUMMY
Cut 1 in white felt

CLEMENTINE CAT

UPPER FRONT HEAD
Cut 1 in marmalade felt

EYE
BACKING
Cut 2 in white felt

NOSE
Cut 1 in black felt

CLEMENTINE CAT

CLEMENTINE CAT

BODY
Cut 2 in marmalade felt

CLEMENTINE CAT

EAR
Cut 2 in marmalade felt
Cut 2 in print fabric

CLEMENTINE CAT

FOOTPAD
Cut 2 in print fabric

THE PATTERNS

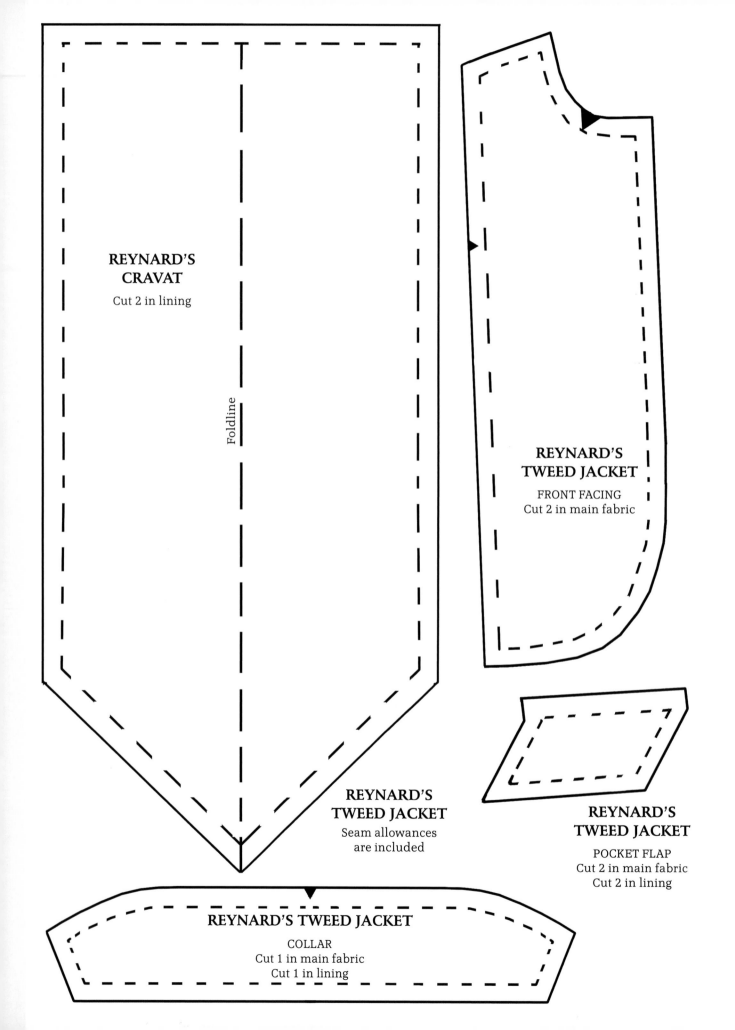

REYNARD'S CRAVAT

Cut 2 in lining

Foldline

REYNARD'S TWEED JACKET

FRONT FACING
Cut 2 in main fabric

REYNARD'S TWEED JACKET

Seam allowances are included

REYNARD'S TWEED JACKET

POCKET FLAP
Cut 2 in main fabric
Cut 2 in lining

REYNARD'S TWEED JACKET

COLLAR
Cut 1 in main fabric
Cut 1 in lining

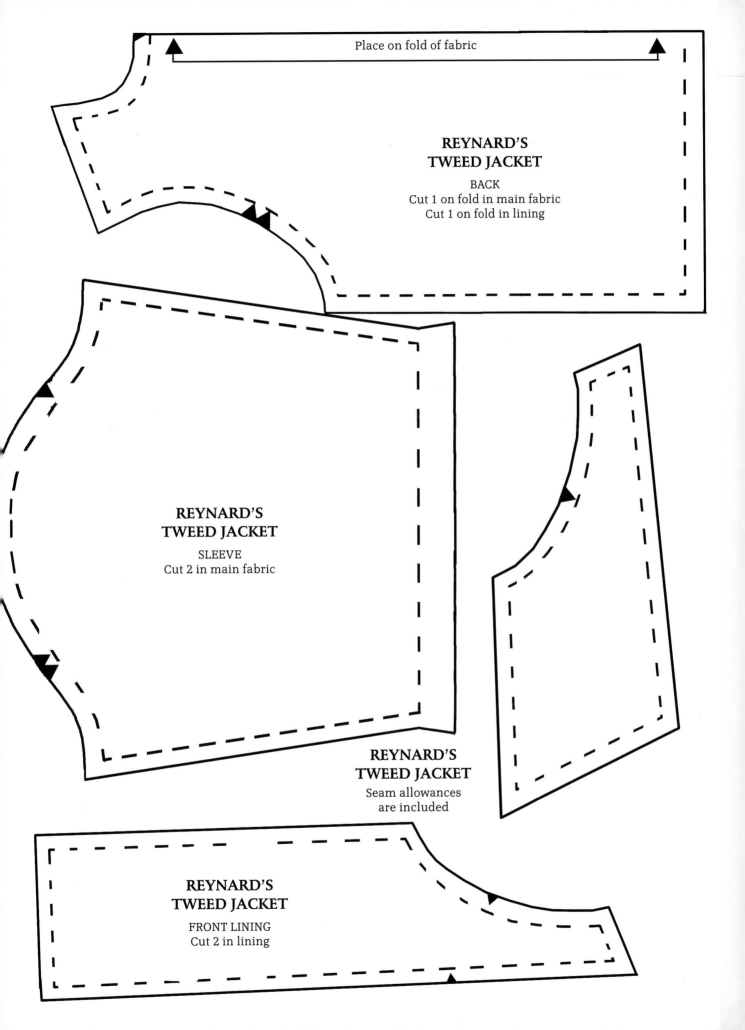

Place on fold of fabric

**REYNARD'S
TWEED JACKET**

BACK
Cut 1 on fold in main fabric
Cut 1 on fold in lining

**REYNARD'S
TWEED JACKET**

SLEEVE
Cut 2 in main fabric

**REYNARD'S
TWEED JACKET**

Seam allowances
are included

**REYNARD'S
TWEED JACKET**

FRONT LINING
Cut 2 in lining

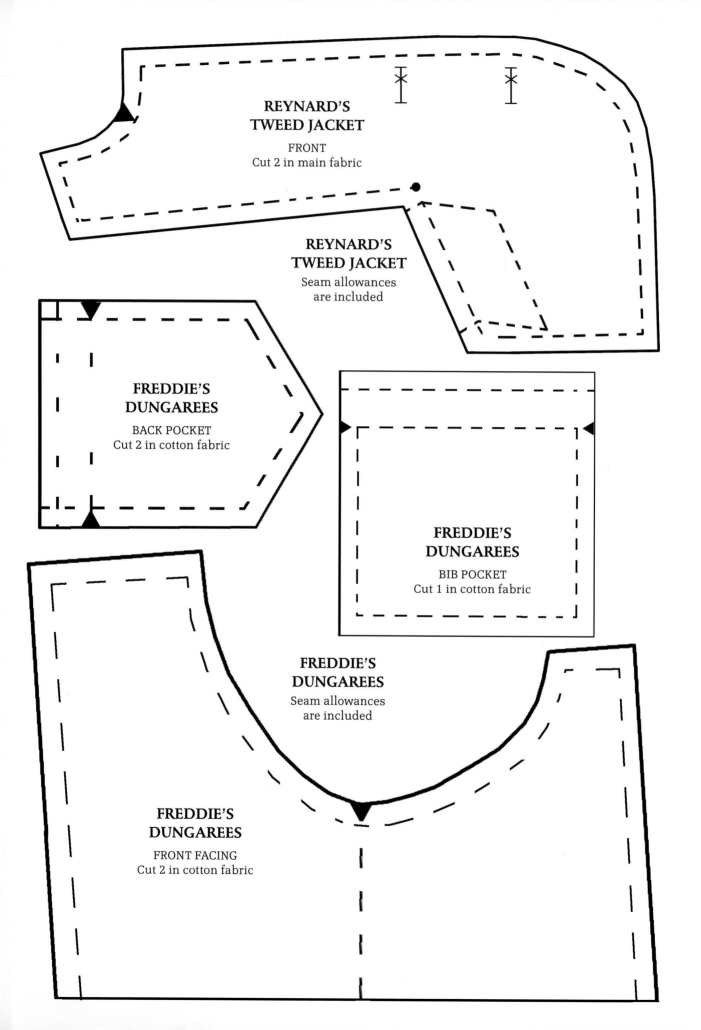

**REYNARD'S
TWEED JACKET**

FRONT
Cut 2 in main fabric

**REYNARD'S
TWEED JACKET**

Seam allowances
are included

**FREDDIE'S
DUNGAREES**

BACK POCKET
Cut 2 in cotton fabric

**FREDDIE'S
DUNGAREES**

BIB POCKET
Cut 1 in cotton fabric

**FREDDIE'S
DUNGAREES**

Seam allowances
are included

**FREDDIE'S
DUNGAREES**

FRONT FACING
Cut 2 in cotton fabric

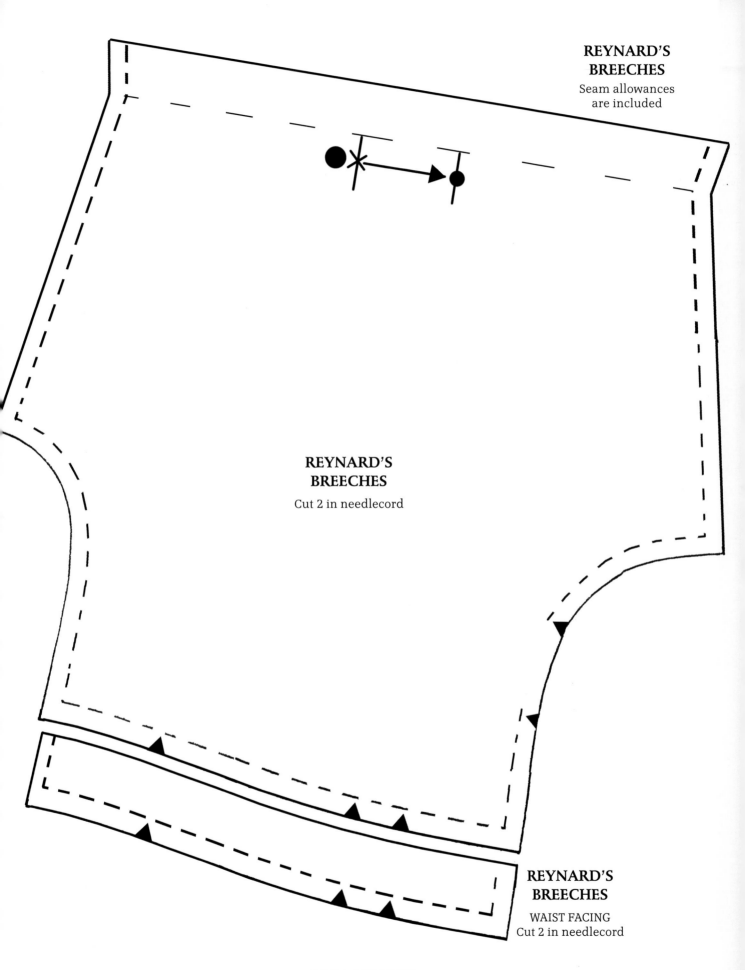

REYNARD'S BREECHES
Seam allowances are included

REYNARD'S BREECHES

Cut 2 in needlecord

REYNARD'S BREECHES

WAIST FACING
Cut 2 in needlecord

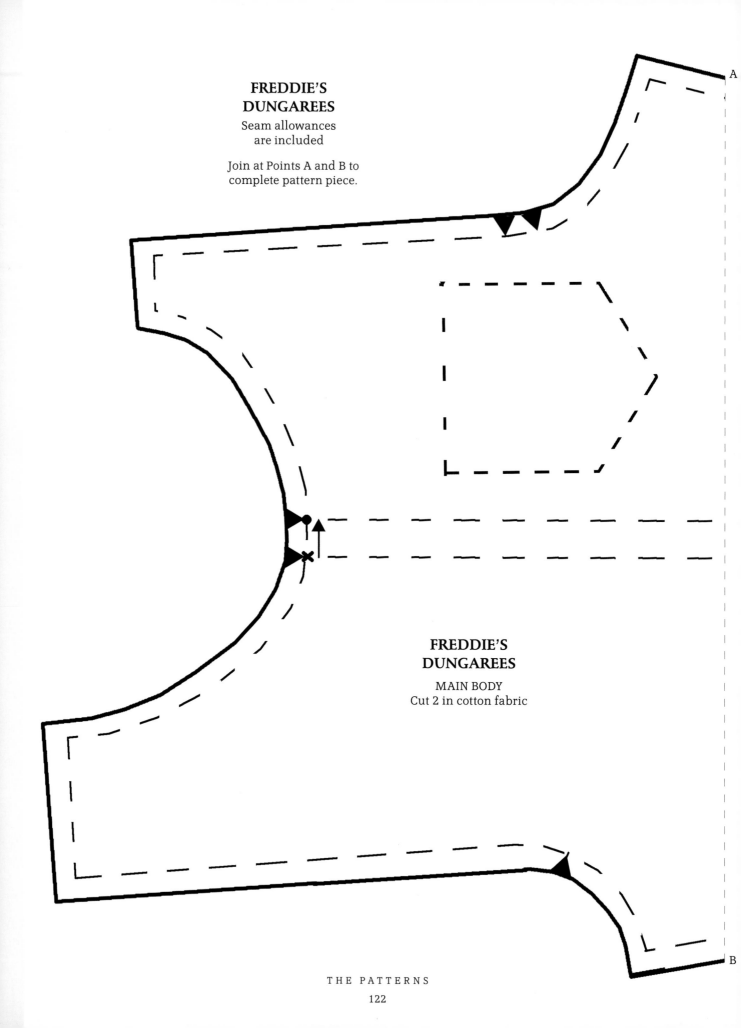

**FREDDIE'S
DUNGAREES**
Seam allowances
are included

Join at Points A and B to
complete pattern piece.

**FREDDIE'S
DUNGAREES**

MAIN BODY
Cut 2 in cotton fabric

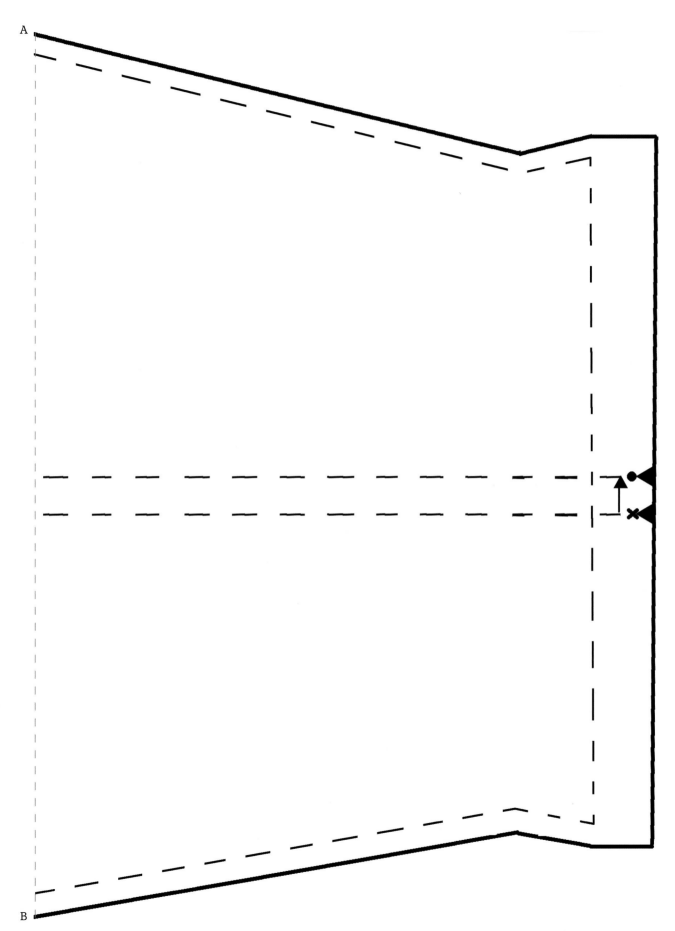

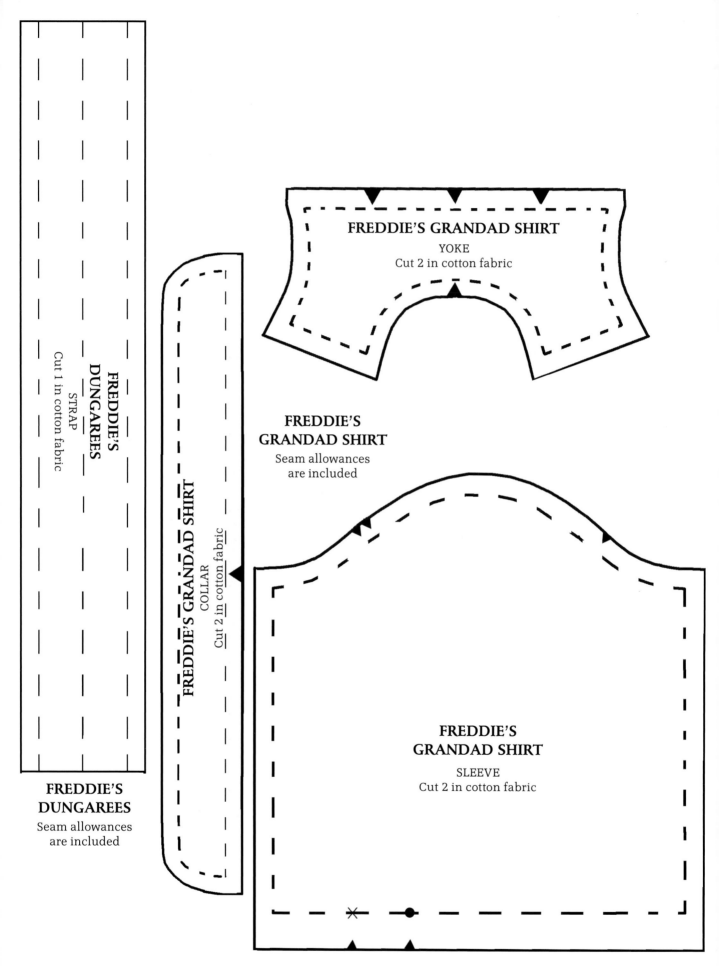

FREDDIE'S DUNGAREES

STRAP
Cut 1 in cotton fabric

FREDDIE'S GRANDAD SHIRT

YOKE
Cut 2 in cotton fabric

FREDDIE'S
GRANDAD SHIRT

Seam allowances
are included

FREDDIE'S GRANDAD SHIRT

COLLAR
Cut 2 in cotton fabric

FREDDIE'S
GRANDAD SHIRT

SLEEVE
Cut 2 in cotton fabric

FREDDIE'S
DUNGAREES

Seam allowances
are included

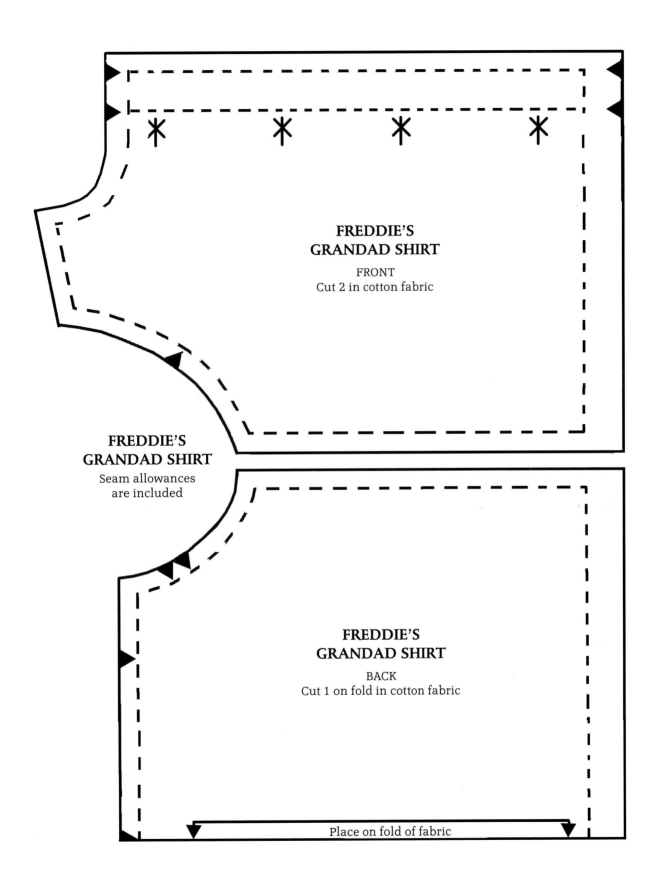

FREDDIE'S
GRANDAD SHIRT

FRONT
Cut 2 in cotton fabric

FREDDIE'S
GRANDAD SHIRT

Seam allowances
are included

FREDDIE'S
GRANDAD SHIRT

BACK
Cut 1 on fold in cotton fabric

Place on fold of fabric

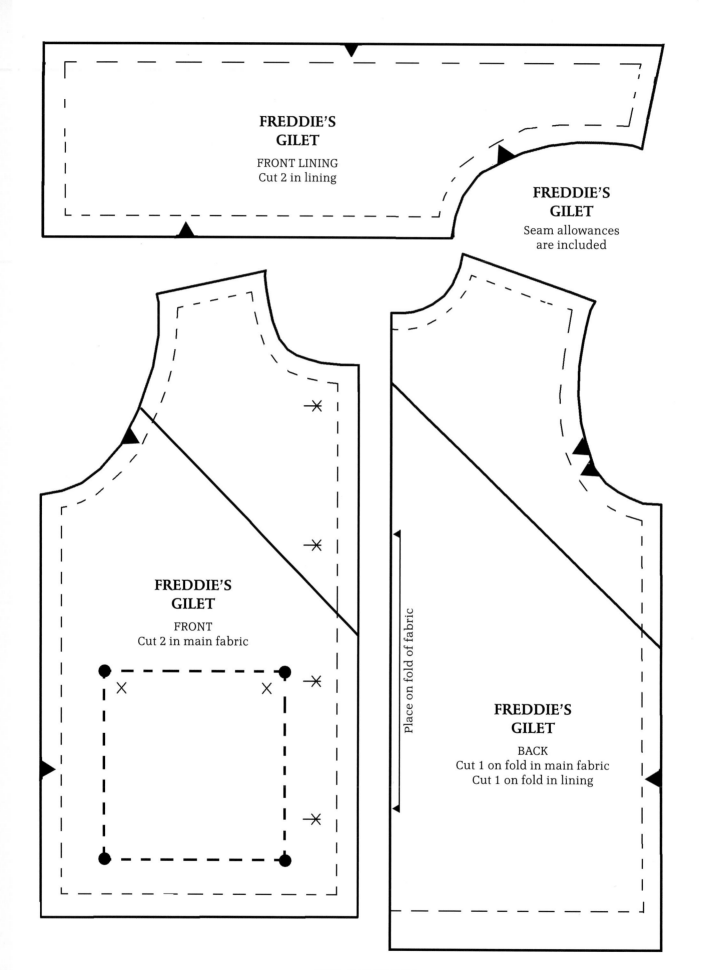

FREDDIE'S GILET

FRONT LINING
Cut 2 in lining

FREDDIE'S GILET

Seam allowances are included

FREDDIE'S GILET

FRONT
Cut 2 in main fabric

Place on fold of fabric

FREDDIE'S GILET

BACK
Cut 1 on fold in main fabric
Cut 1 on fold in lining

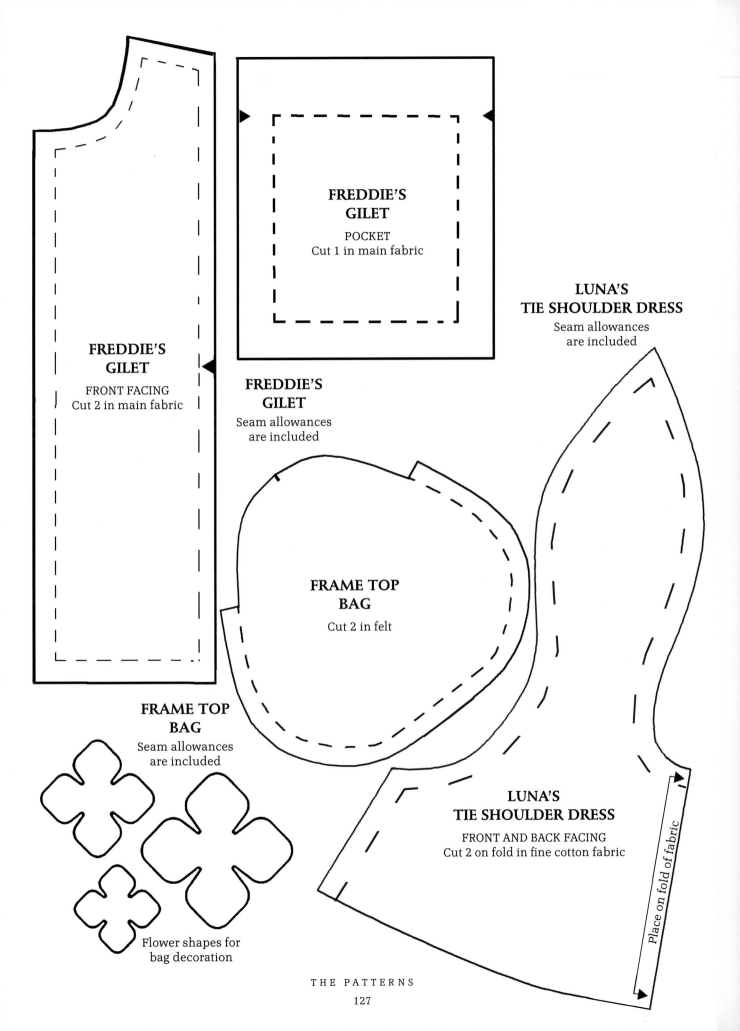

FREDDIE'S GILET

POCKET
Cut 1 in main fabric

LUNA'S TIE SHOULDER DRESS

Seam allowances
are included

FREDDIE'S GILET

FRONT FACING
Cut 2 in main fabric

FREDDIE'S GILET

Seam allowances
are included

FRAME TOP BAG

Cut 2 in felt

FRAME TOP BAG

Seam allowances
are included

LUNA'S TIE SHOULDER DRESS

FRONT AND BACK FACING
Cut 2 on fold in fine cotton fabric

Place on fold of fabric

Flower shapes for
bag decoration

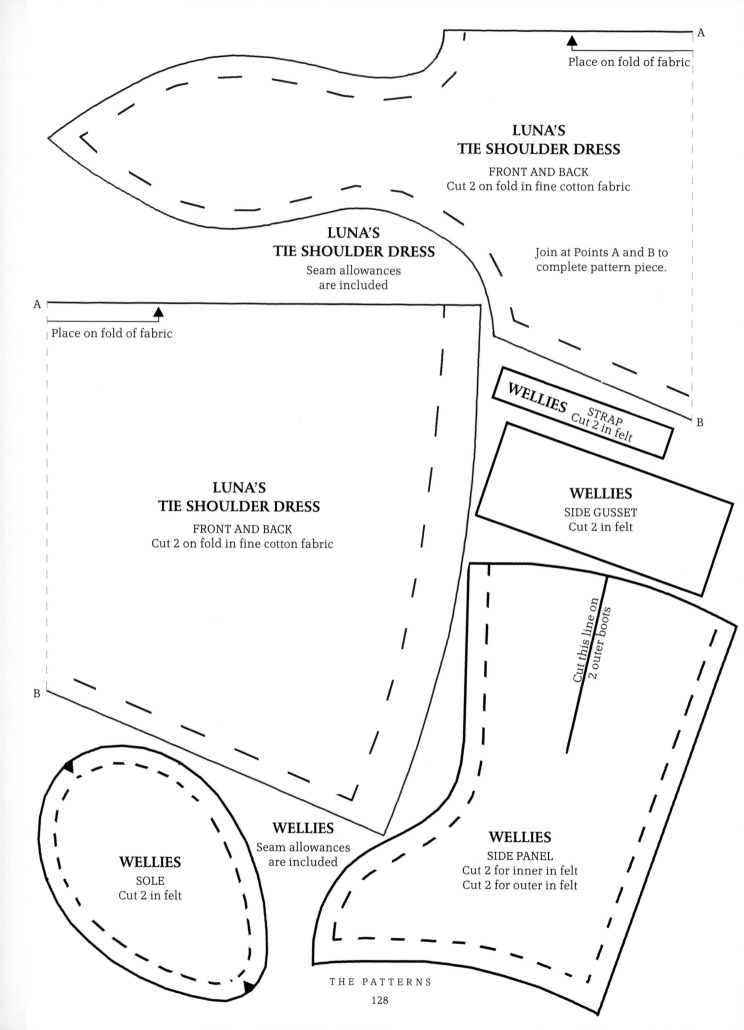

LUNA'S TIE SHOULDER DRESS

FRONT AND BACK
Cut 2 on fold in fine cotton fabric

Join at Points A and B to complete pattern piece.

A

Place on fold of fabric

LUNA'S TIE SHOULDER DRESS

Seam allowances are included

A

Place on fold of fabric

LUNA'S TIE SHOULDER DRESS

FRONT AND BACK
Cut 2 on fold in fine cotton fabric

B

B

WELLIES STRAP
Cut 2 in felt

WELLIES

SIDE GUSSET
Cut 2 in felt

Cut this line on 2 outer boots

WELLIES

Seam allowances are included

WELLIES

SIDE PANEL
Cut 2 for inner in felt
Cut 2 for outer in felt

WELLIES

SOLE
Cut 2 in felt

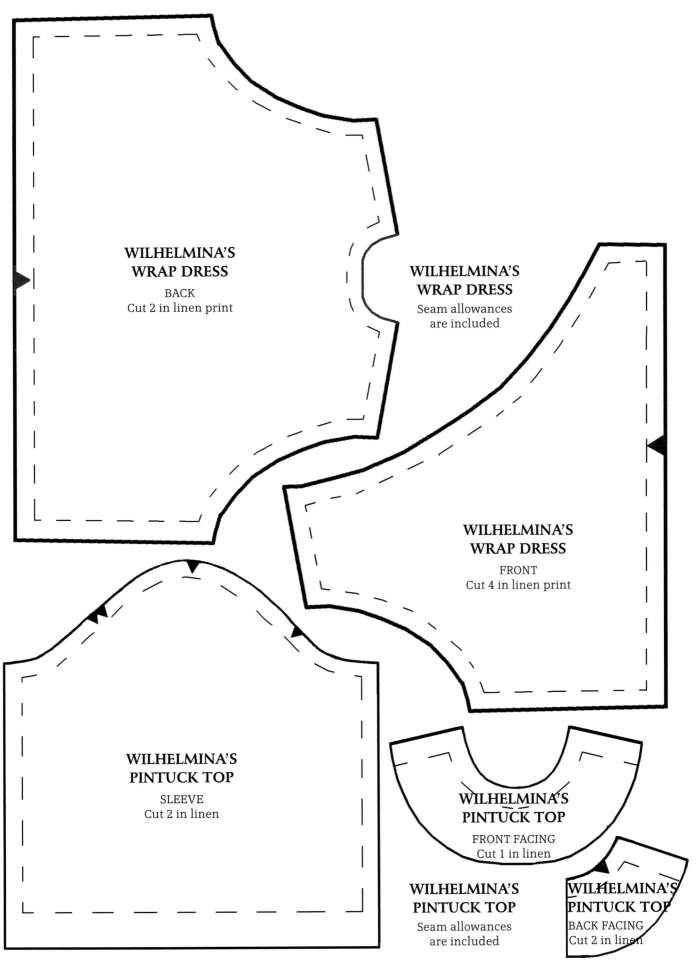

WILHELMINA'S
WRAP DRESS

BACK
Cut 2 in linen print

WILHELMINA'S
WRAP DRESS

Seam allowances
are included

WILHELMINA'S
WRAP DRESS

FRONT
Cut 4 in linen print

WILHELMINA'S
PINTUCK TOP

SLEEVE
Cut 2 in linen

WILHELMINA'S
PINTUCK TOP

FRONT FACING
Cut 1 in linen

WILHELMINA'S
PINTUCK TOP

Seam allowances
are included

WILHELMINA'S
PINTUCK TOP

BACK FACING
Cut 2 in linen

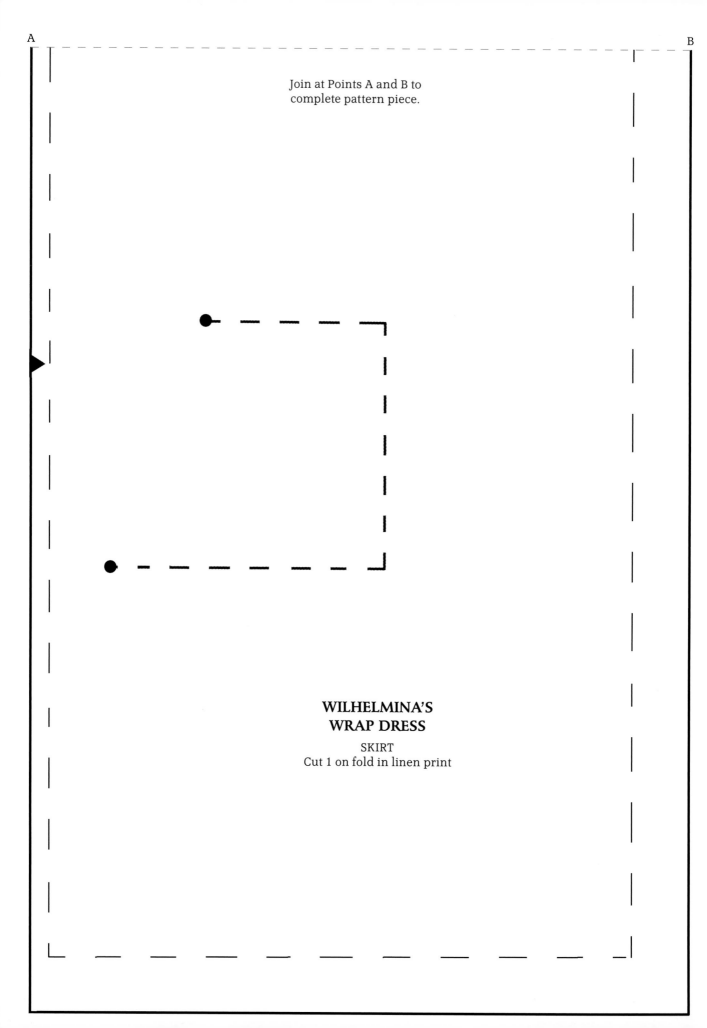

A   B

Join at Points A and B to
complete pattern piece.

**WILHELMINA'S
WRAP DRESS**

SKIRT
Cut 1 on fold in linen print

A   B

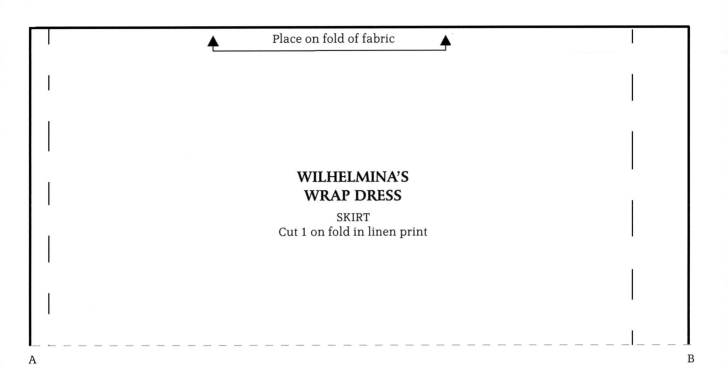

Place on fold of fabric

**WILHELMINA'S
WRAP DRESS**

SKIRT
Cut 1 on fold in linen print

A

B

LUNA'S NIGHTIE

Seam allowances
are included

LUNA'S NIGHTIE

YOKE
Cut 2 in cotton print fabric

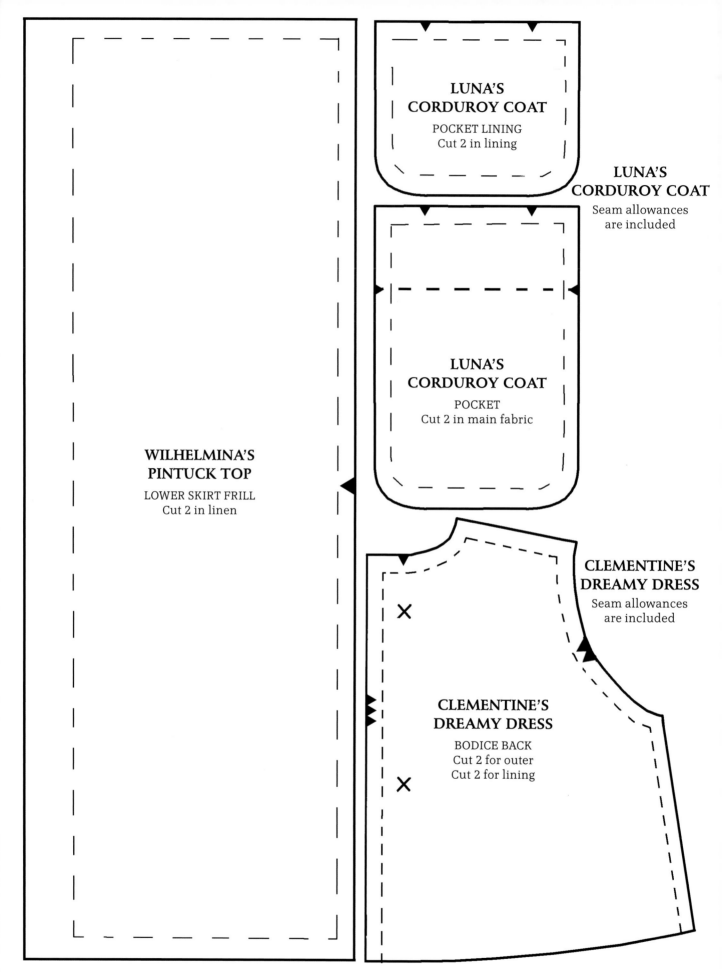

LUNA'S CORDUROY COAT

POCKET LINING
Cut 2 in lining

LUNA'S CORDUROY COAT

Seam allowances
are included

LUNA'S CORDUROY COAT

POCKET
Cut 2 in main fabric

WILHELMINA'S PINTUCK TOP

LOWER SKIRT FRILL
Cut 2 in linen

CLEMENTINE'S DREAMY DRESS

Seam allowances
are included

CLEMENTINE'S DREAMY DRESS

BODICE BACK
Cut 2 for outer
Cut 2 for lining

THE PATTERNS

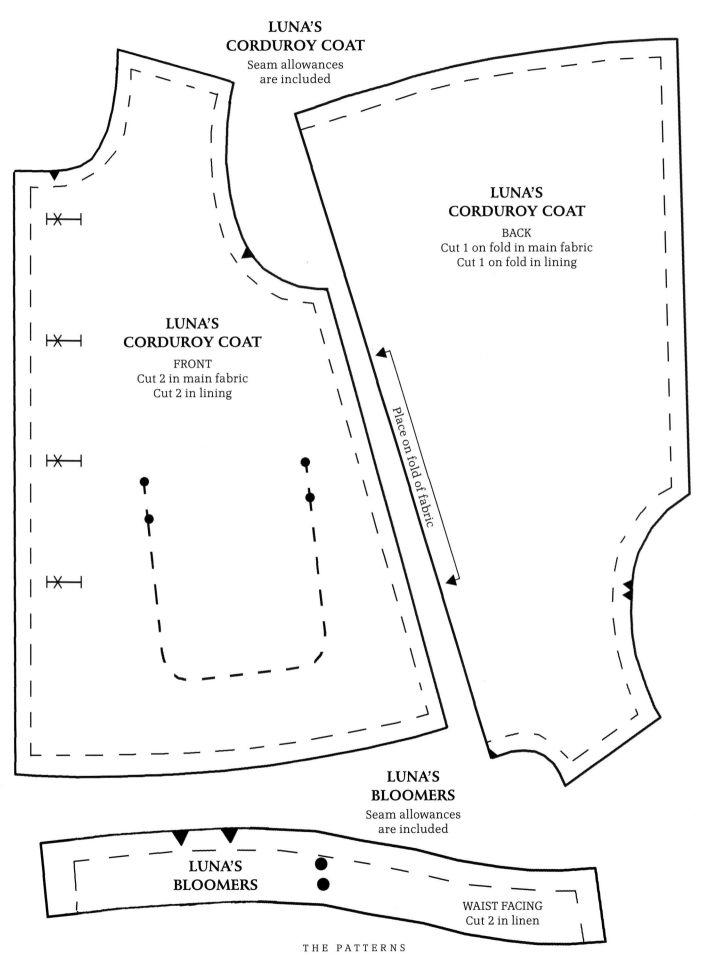

**LUNA'S
CORDUROY COAT**

Seam allowances
are included

**LUNA'S
CORDUROY COAT**

BACK
Cut 1 on fold in main fabric
Cut 1 on fold in lining

Place on fold of fabric

**LUNA'S
CORDUROY COAT**

FRONT
Cut 2 in main fabric
Cut 2 in lining

**LUNA'S
BLOOMERS**

Seam allowances
are included

**LUNA'S
BLOOMERS**

WAIST FACING
Cut 2 in linen

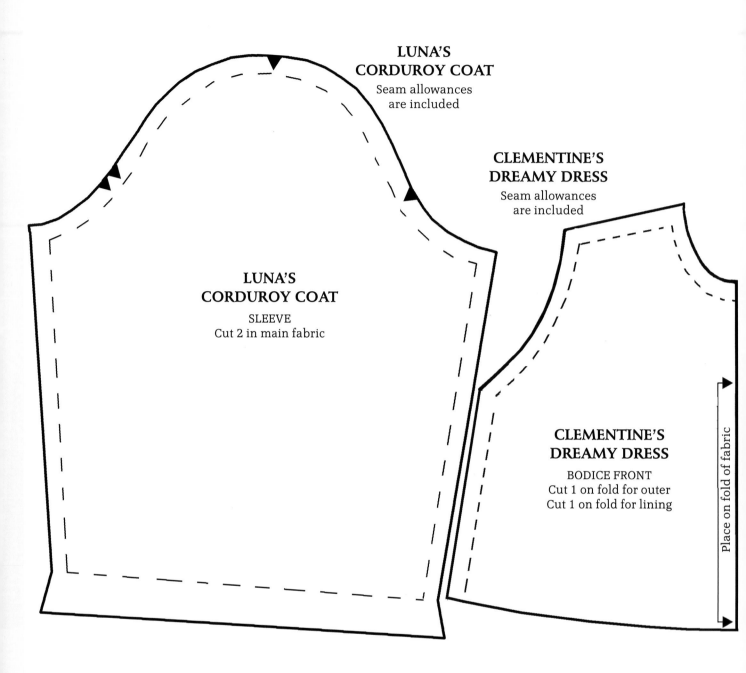

**LUNA'S
CORDUROY COAT**
Seam allowances
are included

**CLEMENTINE'S
DREAMY DRESS**
Seam allowances
are included

**LUNA'S
CORDUROY COAT**
SLEEVE
Cut 2 in main fabric

**CLEMENTINE'S
DREAMY DRESS**
BODICE FRONT
Cut 1 on fold for outer
Cut 1 on fold for lining

Place on fold of fabric

A

**LUNA'S
BLOOMERS**
LOWER LEG FRILL
Cut 2 in linen

Join at Points A and B to
complete pattern piece.

B

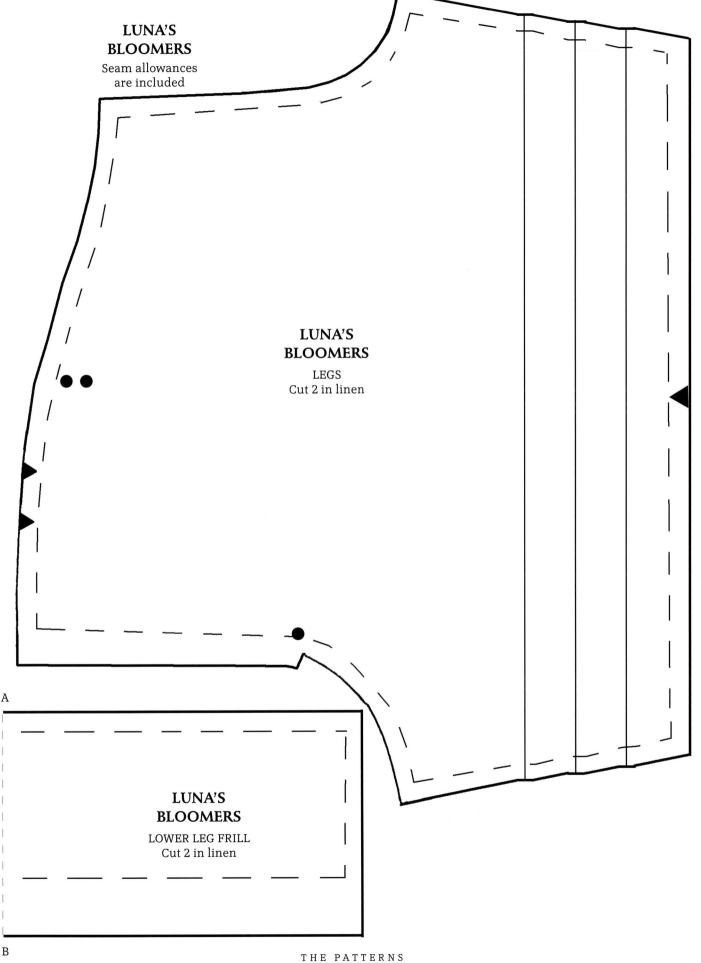

LUNA'S
BLOOMERS

Seam allowances
are included

LUNA'S
BLOOMERS

LEGS
Cut 2 in linen

A

LUNA'S
BLOOMERS

LOWER LEG FRILL
Cut 2 in linen

B

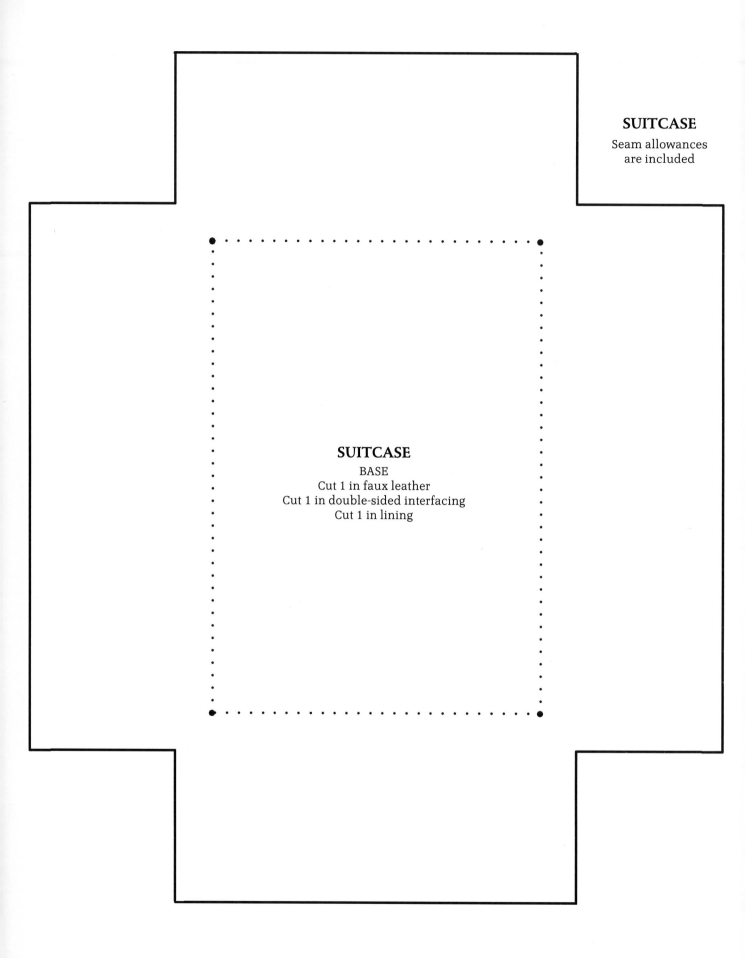

SUITCASE
Seam allowances
are included

SUITCASE
BASE
Cut 1 in faux leather
Cut 1 in double-sided interfacing
Cut 1 in lining

SUITCASE

HANDLE

Cut 1 in faux leather

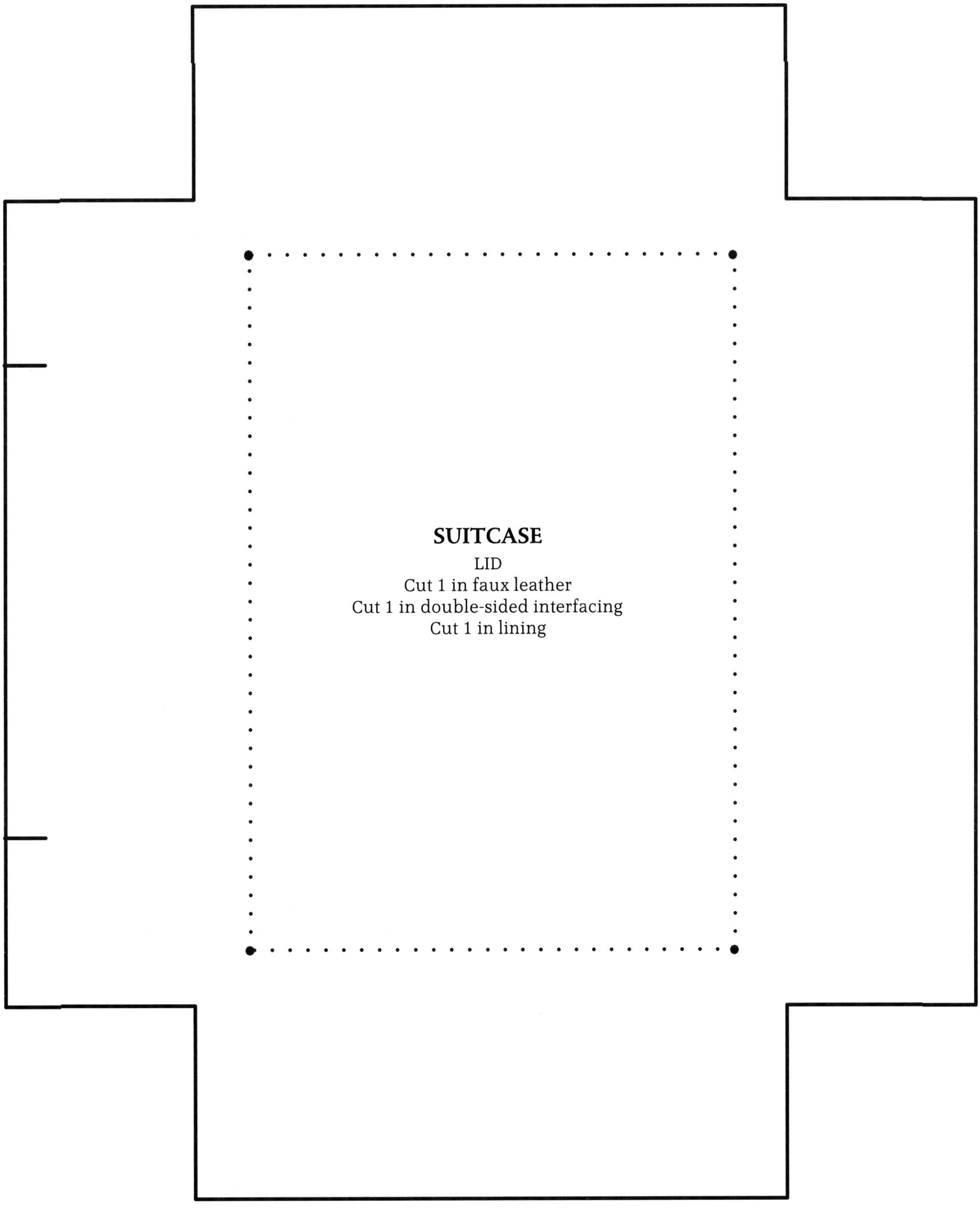

SUITCASE

LID

Cut 1 in faux leather

Cut 1 in double-sided interfacing

Cut 1 in lining

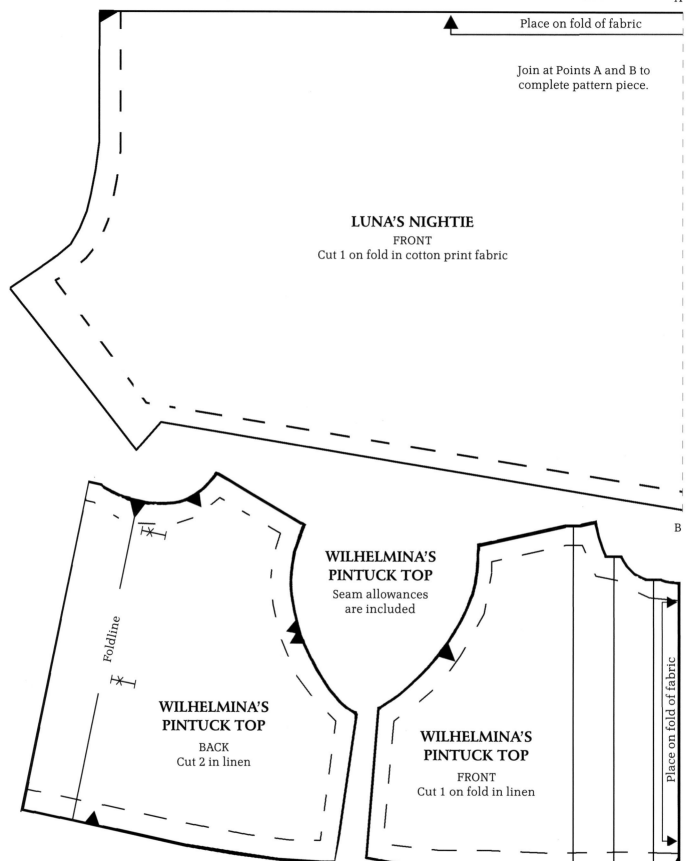

Place on fold of fabric

Join at Points A and B to complete pattern piece.

LUNA'S NIGHTIE
FRONT
Cut 1 on fold in cotton print fabric

B

WILHELMINA'S PINTUCK TOP
Seam allowances are included

Foldline

WILHELMINA'S PINTUCK TOP
BACK
Cut 2 in linen

WILHELMINA'S PINTUCK TOP
FRONT
Cut 1 on fold in linen

Place on fold of fabric

THE PATTERNS

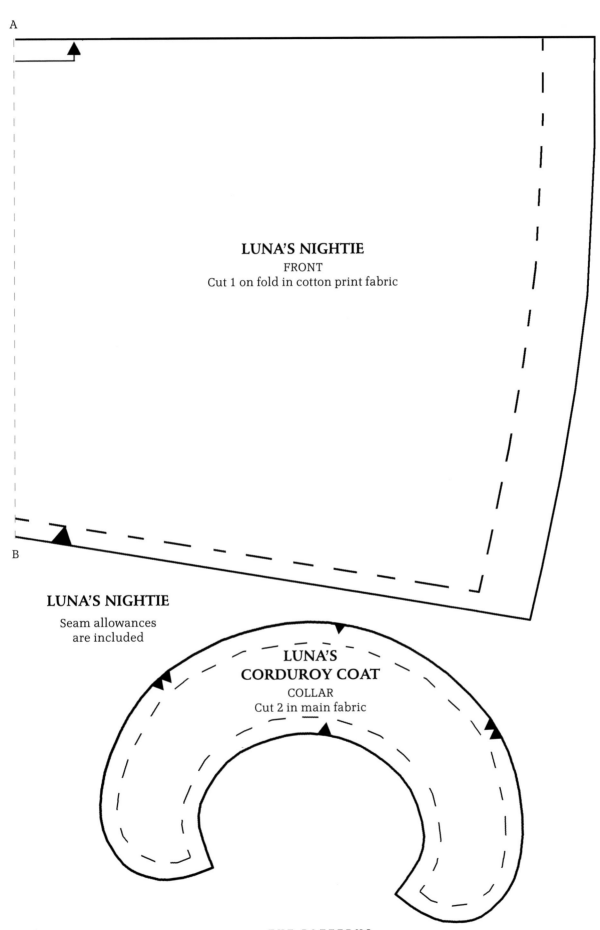

A

LUNA'S NIGHTIE
FRONT
Cut 1 on fold in cotton print fabric

B

LUNA'S NIGHTIE

Seam allowances
are included

**LUNA'S
CORDUROY COAT**
COLLAR
Cut 2 in main fabric

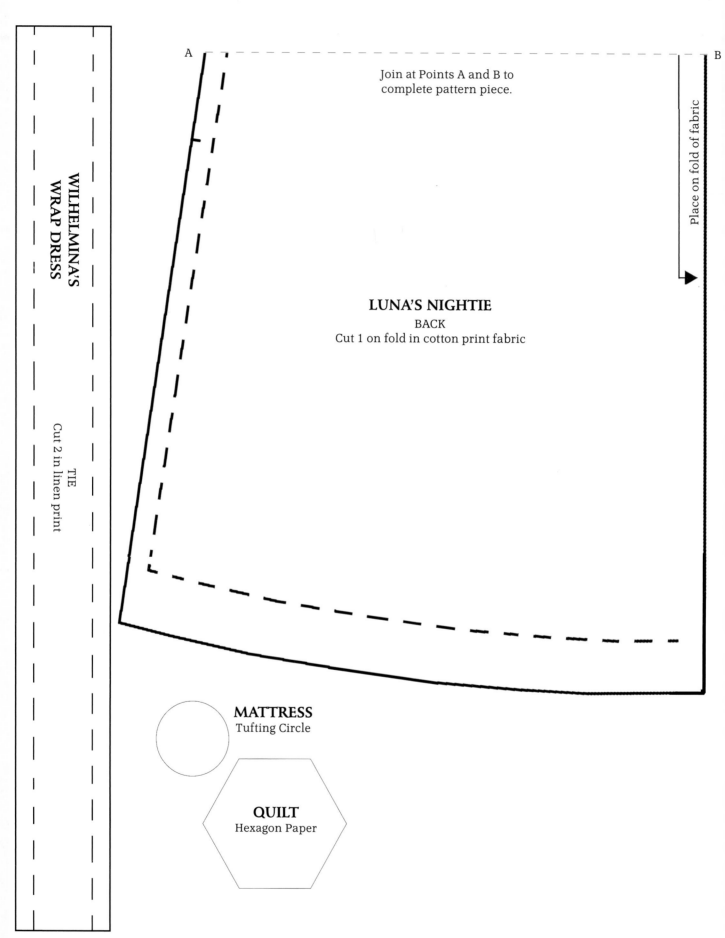

WILHELMINA'S
WRAP DRESS

TIE
Cut 2 in linen print

A

B

Join at Points A and B to
complete pattern piece.

Place on fold of fabric

LUNA'S NIGHTIE
BACK
Cut 1 on fold in cotton print fabric

MATTRESS
Tufting Circle

QUILT
Hexagon Paper

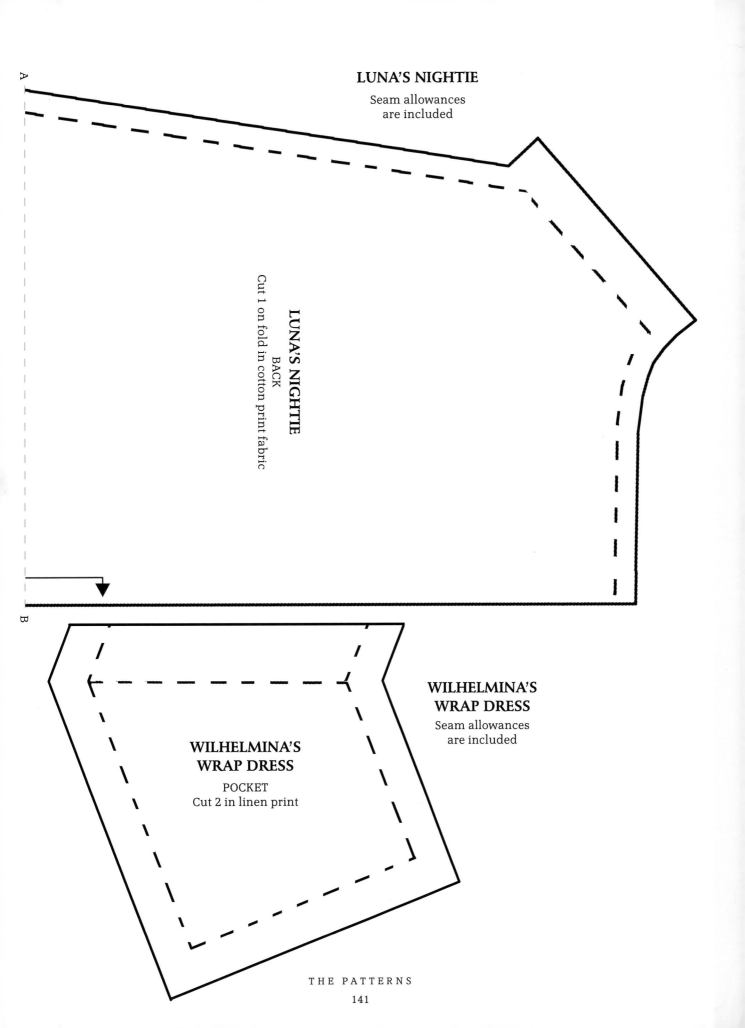

LUNA'S NIGHTIE

Seam allowances
are included

A

LUNA'S NIGHTIE
BACK
Cut 1 on fold in cotton print fabric

B

**WILHELMINA'S
WRAP DRESS**

Seam allowances
are included

**WILHELMINA'S
WRAP DRESS**

POCKET
Cut 2 in linen print

SUPPLIERS

I always like to consider what I have already before I shop, as that way my purchases have more value. So have a look in your stash, consider old clothes that could have a new life, or browse your nearest charity shop. There are a huge amount of suppliers online, and you can also look in your local haberdashery stores for supplies. Most supplies can be bought from coolcrafting.co.uk either individually or as kits for each project.

COOLCRAFTING

7 Stramongate, Kendal, LA9 4BH

Tel: 01539 724099
Email: info@coolcrafting.co.uk
www.coolcrafting.co.uk

For a wide range of contemporary craft products, including sewing supplies, print fabrics, wool felt, buttons, ribbons, trims, braids, lace and bias binding (including lace-edged).

There are some supplies that aren't stocked by CoolCrafting but which you may like to consider, as follows:

Tweed
www.fabricaffair.co.uk
Beautiful washed Irish Donegal tweeds from our good friend Margaret Lee.

Liberty Fabrics
www.libertylondon.com
The home of Tana Lawn prints, which are a perfect scale for Luna's little world.

www.alicecaroline.co.uk
Liberty print specialists from Alice Garrett.

Reused Fabrics
www.wornandwashedfabrics.com
If you want to achieve a vintage look to your new sewing, take a look at Kim Porter's wonderful repurposed fabrics.

Toy Stuffing
www.bronteglen.co.uk
A range of stuffing suitable for our projects, from value polyester to amazing 'Best Balled Wool'.

ACKNOWLEDGEMENTS

I had a charmed childhood; so many of my memories are truly magical. My mum would sew with me, teach me the names of flowers, birds, plants. Still going home to her makes me feel youthful – Joan Peel, you are my inspiration and I thank you! Grace, Callum, Nathan – my children – for making my heart swell.

Anthony – for always asking 'How can I help?' and maybe not so much for 'There's no bl**dy price on this!' To my sister, Deborah Sims and her husband Tony – who have turned up when I've needed them, and been more helpful than I deserve. To all the girls who work for me compiling kits, or selling our brand of beautiful – here is a big thank you. To Sarah Callard, Acquisitions Editor of both books, for being determined and soothing all at once. And of course, to our loyal, supportive customers, Luna lovers of the universe – your words, makes and friendship mean the world.

ABOUT THE AUTHOR

CoolCrafting founder Sarah Peel has a lifetime of experience within the fashion industry. Sensing a movement back to 'handmade', Sarah set up the business in 2011, providing inspirational workshops, supplies and kits for sewing and crafting. She lives on the edge of the English Lake District in Hincaster, Cumbria with her family, dog and cat. Luna was born on a dark, Christmassy night in 2013 and is now a huge part of the business. Of course, Luna needed some company in her world and she was followed by Reynard, Mae, Clementine, Freddie and Wilhelmina – in that order. As well as selling online, Sarah has a shop in Kendal, Cumbria.

www.coolcrafting.co.uk

INDEX

A DAVID AND CHARLES BOOK
© David and Charles, Ltd 2018

David and Charles is an imprint of David and Charles, Ltd
Suite A, Tourism House, Pynes Hill, Exeter, EX2 5WS

Text and Designs © Sarah Peel 2018
Layout and Photography © David and Charles, Ltd 2018

First published in the UK and USA in 2018

ISBN-13: 978-1-4463-0701-4 paperback

ISBN-13: 978-1-4463-7660-7 EPUB

Printed in the UK by Pureprint for:
David and Charles, Ltd
Suite A, Tourism House, Pynes Hill, Exeter, EX2 5WS

10 9

Content Director: Ame Verso
Acquisitions Editor: Sarah Callard
Managing Editor: Jeni Hennah
Project Editor: Wendy Ward
Proofreader: Cheryl Brown
Design and Art Direction: Prudence Rogers
Photographer: Jason Jenkins
Production Manager: Beverley Richardson

David and Charles publishes high-quality books on a wide range of subjects. For more information visit www.davidandcharles.com.

Layout of the digital edition of this book may vary depending on reader hardware and display settings.